W9-ACA-797

ACCOUNTS,
EXCUSES,
and
APOLOGIES

SUNY Series in Speech Communication
Dudley D. Cahn, Editor

ACCOUNTS, EXCUSES, and APOLOGIES

A Theory of Image Restoration Strategies

WILLIAM L. BENOIT

State University of New York Press

Published by
State University of New York Press, Albany

For information, address State University of New York Press,
State University Plaza, Albany, N.Y., 12246

Production by Bernadine Dawes
Marketing by Dana Yanulavich

Library Of Congress Cataloging-in-Publication Data

Benoit, William L.
    Accounts, excuses, and apologies : a theory of image restoration
discourse / William L. Benoit.
        p.   cm.–(SUNY series in speech communication)
    Includes bibliographical references and index.
    ISBN 0-7914-2185-6 – ISBN 0-7914-2186-4 (pbk.)
    1. Discourse analysis. 2. Verbal self-defense. 3. Rhetorical
criticism. I. Title. II. Series.
P302.85.B46 1995
401'.41–dc20   94-31901
                                                                    CIP

10 9 8 7 6 5 4 3 2 1

CONTENTS

PREFACE

The central theme in this book is that human beings engage in recurrent patterns of communicative behavior designed to reduce, redress, or avoid damage to their reputation (or face or image) from perceived wrong-doing. Complaints are routinely leveled at people in all walks of life for all sorts of alleged misbehavior; accordingly, we are repeatedly faced with situations that impel us to explain or justify our behavior, to offer excuses or apologies for those aspects of our behavior that offend and provoke reproach from those around us. Our face, image, or reputation is a valuable commodity. We not only desire a healthy image of ourselves, but we want others to think favorably of us as well. Hence, the communicative activity of excuse-making or image restoration deserves serious study not only because it pervades social life, but also because it serves an important function in our lives, by helping to restore our precious reputations.

Over ten years ago I analyzed President Nixon's Watergate rhetoric, in which he attempted to defend his image (and his presidency) against contamination from the Watergate incident (Benoit, 1982). Subsequently, Jim Lindsey and I studied Tylenol's response to the poisoning of their pain-reliever capsules (Benoit & Lindsey, 1987). Next, I wrote a chapter analyzing Senator Kennedy's Chappaquid-dick speech (Benoit, 1988). This was quite a challenge for me, because I studied rhetorical criticism with Dave Ling, who had written an article on this speech in 1970 that greatly impressed me. Paul Gullifor, Dan Panici, and I analyzed President Reagan's discourse on the Iran-Contra affair (Benoit, Gullifor, & Panici, 1991). A common thread had emerged in these studies: they all concerned rhetorical attempts to restore the person's image after being the target of blame.

As I reflected on this topic, I began to realize that discourse that apologizes, makes excuses, or otherwise attempts to restore a favorable image is pervasive. My reading of the rhetorical literature led me to conclude that, while there were several useful treatments of this topic (e.g., Rosenfield, 1968; Ware & Linkugel, 1973; Burke, 1970), no one had developed a comprehensive theory of excuses and apologies in public discourse. About this time my wife, Pam, called to my attention Scott and Lyman's classic article on accounts, which led me to examine the literature on accounts. Although communication scholars are not shy about borrowing from related areas (e.g., Ware and Linkugel [1973] derived their theory of apologia from Robert Abelson's [1959] strategies for conflict resolution), I thought this work on accounts had gone undeservedly unnoticed in the rhetorical realm of our discipline.

At this point I decided it would be desirable to develop an integrated or general theory of image restoration, drawing heavily on both rhetorical criticism of apologia and work on accounts. A preliminary version appeared in our criticism of Reagan's Iran-Contra rhetoric (Benoit, Gullifor, & Panici, 1991). My reading of the rhetorical literature, presented in chapter 2, reveals that none of the three major theories I review (Rosenfield, Ware & Linkugel, and Burke) made use of one another's ideas, and there were few attempts by subsequent authors to integrate them. I also believed that the presentation of this theory would be more effective if several illustrative applications were to accompany it. These considerations prompted this book.

While I worked on this book, I continued to work on related projects. Susan Brinson and I investigated AT&T's response to their long-distance service interruption in New York City (Benoit & Brinson, 1994). Dawn Nill and I analyzed Oliver Stone's defense of himself and his film, *JFK* (Benoit & Nill, 1994). Kerby Anderson and I analyzed *Murphy Brown*'s response to the attack from Dan Quayle (Benoit & Anderson, 1994). Robert Hanczor and I analyzed Tanya Harding's response to charges of involvement in the attack on Nancy Kerrigan (Benoit & Hanczor, in press) With Bruce Dorries, I examined persuasive attack by *Dateline NBC* on Wal-Mart (Benoit & Dorries, 1994). Shirley Drew and I conducted experimental work on image restoration strategies (Benoit & Drew, 1994). The ideas in these works inevitably spilled over into the book, enriching it.

Although I characterize this as a "general theory" of image restoration, I don't intend this label to imply that I believe I have articulated an exhaustive discussion of everything of interest concerning excuses, apologies, and accounts. The complexity of human behavior, the pervasiveness of this activity, and the diversity of scholarly interests prevent me from making the claim that this theory is complete. I have attempted to describe the major strategies for dealing with actual, perceived, or potential damage to one's reputation, develop a general theory of image restoration, and to illustrate this approach with several case studies. I label it a general theory of image restoration (as opposed to a comprehensive theory) because it has a broader scope than existing treatments (especially in the rhetorical literature). Although the applications in this book all concern public attempts to restore images, I see no conceptual reason for limiting this theory to that domain of discourse.

The book begins with an introduction that develops the argument that apology/excuse/account behavior is a common feature of human behavior. This is followed by two review chapters, one devoted to rhetorical approaches to image restoration and one to accounts. These analyses culminate in chapter 4, which presents my general theory of image restoration discourse. Then, four chapters illustrate this theory through applications to corporate apologetic discourse (chapters on the cola wars of Coke and Pepsi, the Exxon *Valdez* oil spill, and the Union Carbide Bhopal gas leak) and political apologetic discourse (a chapter on President Nixon's preemptive apology for his invasion of Cambodia). The last chapter offers concluding remarks and attempts to draw together some of the threads that emerge from these (and related) applications.

This book has been interesting and fun to write. During the process, I became acutely aware of my own excuse-making. For example, this book took longer to complete than I predicted, and, of course, I made excuses to my editor and publisher (who were very understanding). I also began to scrutinize the excuses offered to me by students, colleagues, and friends. These episodes only served to strengthen my conviction that I was studying an important and pervasive social phenomenon.

I would like to thank a number of people for their contributions to this project. First, I studied rhetorical criticism with Dave Ling, John Schmidt, and Bernard Brock, and they all influenced my subsequent work in this area. Coursework with George Ziegelmueller (on argument) and Jim Measell (on rhetorical theory) was also important to my intellectual development. Coauthors I have worked with over the years (e.g., Jim Lindsey, Paul Gullifor, Dan Panici, Susan Brinson, Shirley Drew, Dawn Nill, Bruce Dorries,

Kerby Anderson, Robert Hanczor, Bill Wells, and Anne Czerwinski), students, other teachers, and colleagues have influenced my views of rhetoric generally and image restoration discourse specifically. Dudley Cahn, series editor of the SUNY Series in Speech Communication, encouraged my work on this project and offered many useful suggestions. Priscilla Ross, SUNY Press editor, and Bernadine Dawes, my production editor, were also very helpful. Three anonymous reviewers for SUNY Press made useful suggestions. My wife, Pam, not only steered me toward sociological accounts of accounts, but also gave me conceptual advice. She also read preliminary drafts and made helpful suggestions on the book, as did Dale Hample. I am grateful for their insightful comments. My delightful daughter, Jennifer, not only put up with my excuses as I worked on this project but also offered a number of interesting ones of her own for me to consider.

1   Introduction

Human beings frequently must attempt to restore their reputations after alleged or suspected wrong-doing. This is inevitable for at least four reasons. First, we inhabit a world of limited resources: there is only so much time, money, equipment, office space, room in classes, computer time, and so forth. Individuals often compete fiercely for these tangible and intangible goods, which means the allocation of these scarce resources often provokes the ire of those who desired a different distribution. Second, circumstances beyond our control sometimes prevent us from meeting our obligations. We become delayed by unexpected traffic and arrive late to meetings; documents or computer files may become lost or corrupted; or a colleague may neglect to inform us that a meeting has been moved up a day. Our behavior is significantly influenced by the people, events, and environment around us, and frequently these factors create problems for us and those who depend on us. Third, human beings are imperfect and make mistakes, some honestly, others guided perhaps too often by our self-interests. We may forget to bring a report to a meeting or to stop and buy milk on the way home from work; a self-employed individual may send the IRS an insufficient quarterly tax payment; or a contractor may substitute cheaper and inferior parts in a building. Alcohol, drugs, or even lack of sleep may cloud our judgment and hinder performance of our duties. Finally, the fact that humans are individuals with different sets of priorities fosters conflict among those with competing goals. These four factors combine to insure that actual or perceived wrong-doing is a recurrent feature of human activity.

When such inevitable (apparent) misbehavior occurs, others are very likely to accuse, attack, berate, blame, censure, condemn, rail against, rebuke, or reproach us or object to our behavior. They may complain about things we said or did, they can carp about things left unsaid or undone, or they might criticize the *way* in which we performed an action or phrased an utterance. Indeed, the simple fact that our language is rich in expressions of disfavor attests to the ubiquity of complaints or persuasive attack.

These attacks on our reputation are serious matters, for our image or reputation is extremely vital to us. Face, image, or reputation not only contributes to a healthy self-image, but it also can create important favorable impressions on others. Conversely, a bad reputation may interfere with our interactions with others. For example, after charges of mismanagement at United Way, groups supported by that charity began to become anxious about its ability to continue fund-raising ("Groups Worry," 1992). Similarly, after a segment of CBS's *60 Minutes* that criticized the use of Alar, apple growers in Washington were upset and initiated legal proceedings against the network ("CBS Being Sued," 1990). Hence, attacks on one's image can be very serious concerns, and most people recognize the importance of these threats to reputation.

Those who believe that their face or reputation has been injured or even threatened are unlikely to ignore these perils. When our image is threatened, we feel compelled to offer explanations, defenses, justifications, rationalizations, apologies, or excuses for our behavior. This book investigates verbal responses to perceived damage to reputation—image restoration strategies— because threats to image are pervasive, reputation is important, and discourse has the power to restore face. This first chapter provides a backdrop for the remainder of this book. First, it offers anecdotal support, drawn from newspaper stories, for the claim that image restoration attempts are a pervasive form of communicative action. Then it provides a brief overview of the remainder of the book.

Defensive communicative acts adopt a variety of stances. One strategy for avoiding blame is denial. For example, after the Missouri state attorney general's office charged Show Me Furniture with deceptive advertising, this business simply denied that its ads were deceptive (Bennish, 1992). Similarly, Christian Laettner, leading scorer on Duke University's NCAA champion basketball team, denied that he had violated his amateur standing ("Laettner Denies," 1992). Governor Jerry Brown rejected allegations that his home had been the scene for drug parties, labeling the attack as "a tissue of false, malicious and absurd allegations" ("Brown Dismisses," 1992, p. 1A). Woody Allen denied charges that he had molested two of his adopted children ("Woody Allen Denies," 1992). Thus, a common response to charges of misconduct is simply to deny any and all allegations. If the audience accepts the claim that an accusation is false, damage to the accused's reputation from that attack should be diminished, if not eradicated.

At times, the strategy of denial is reinforced. Following release of a tape indicating that PLO leader Yasser Arafat made derogatory comments about Jews, it was reported that "Arafat Says Tape was Doctored" (1992, p. 4A). In this instance, not only was the charge denied, but an explanation was provided for the apparently incriminating evidence. Some who defend their image with the claim of innocence also shift the blame to the—allegedly—truly guilty party. Basketball coach Paul Westhead, fired after two dismal seasons with the Denver Nuggets, shifted the blame to his personnel: "the players we had were insufficient" ("Westhead Rejects," 1992, p. 2B). After the 1992 riots in Los Angeles, we heard that President "Bush Blames Programs of '60's, '70's" (1992, p. 1A). Following charges of financial misconduct at United Way, William Aramony, former head of United Way, argued that "he was being denied access to evidence that would disprove accusations" of financial misconduct (Barringer, 1992, p. A16). In addition to denying the charges, he alleged that the evidence he needed to prove his innocence was being withheld. Thus, denial may be supplemented with explanations of apparently damaging facts or scapegoating. Again, if the denial (in these cases with additional supporting reasons) is accepted by the audience, the accused's image should be rehabilitated.

Another strategy for dealing with criticism is to respond in kind, attacking accusers. Responding to a political cartoon, Missouri Attorney General Bill Webster attacked the St. Louis *Post-Dispatch* for "race-baiting" ("Webster Blasts," 1992, p. 5A). A high-ranking naval officer fired after the Tailhook sex scandal was not content to accept his dismissal quietly: "Admiral Blasts Back for Inquiry Accusation" (1992, p. 10A). President Bush felt it necessary to reply to criticism of his pardons of six Iran-Contra defendants, calling such commentary "stupid" and "frivolous" (Clymer, 1992, p. A8). Presumably, such counterattacks undermine the credibility and impact of the accusations, thus helping to restore the accused's image. They may also function to shift the audience's attention away from the alleged wrong-doing of the original target to the new prey.

Some charges may be difficult or impossible to deny. However, this does not mean the situation is hopeless: it is possible to admit guilt and still attempt to restore one's reputation. For example, L.A. Police Chief Daryl Gates, after the 1992 riots, "insisted errors occurred in only one area and not citywide" ("Gates Admits," 1992, p. 12A). If this statement is accepted, it should limit the extent of the harm attributable to him, and, presumably, limit the damage to his face. Marge Schott, owner of the Cincinnati Reds baseball team, admitted using the word "nigger" to refer to players, but declared that she didn't know it was considered offensive ("Schott Tries," 1992). Thus, while not denying that she made the remark, she claimed that she had not intended it as an insult. If the injury from the offensive act is not as significant as first believed, the damage to the image of the accused should be limited as well.

Another defensive strategy for dealing with charges of wrong-doing that cannot be denied is to apologize for misconduct. Senator Robert Packwood, responding to charges of sexual harassment, admitted the charges and offered an apology, although he refused to resign ("Packwood Admits," 1992). Similarly, Lawrence Eagleburger, acting secretary of state, apologized for the passport file searches during President Bush's reelection campaign ("Secretary of State," 1992). Japanese Prime Minister Kiichi Miyazawa apologized for Japan's use of Korean women as sex slaves during World War II ("Japan Apologizes," 1992). Russian President Boris Yeltsin apologized for keeping Japanese prisoners of war as slave labor years after World War II was over ("Japanese Get Apology," 1993). Thus, it is possible for those who commit wrongful acts to attempt to repair their reputation with a sincere apology.

In some instances, those accused of wrong-doing will take action to correct the problem. An advertisement by the University of Missouri Hospital implied that it provided better care than the Mayo Clinic. When the Clinic objected to this ad, the University Hospital was forced to take corrective action: "Mayo Clinic Protests University Hospital Ad: Hospital Apologizes, Withdraws Ad for Changes" (Roth, 1991, p. 12A). Here, the hospital stopped running the unacceptable advertisement, which presumably will put it in a more favorable light. After the check-kiting scandal, the House of Representatives adopted reforms to improve its image ("U.S. House," 1992). If the reforms are believed to be appropriate, voters' image of the House should be improved. While MTV denied that its program had causes a five-year-old to set a fire that killed his sister, nevertheless it prohibited references to setting fires on future episodes of the cartoon program *Beavis and Butt-head* ("MTV Bans," 1993). Here, those who have allegedly committed wrong-doings suggest that they have mended their ways.

Following revelations that the Department of State had investigated passport files of Bill Clinton, his mother, and Ross Perot, we learned that "Bush Dismisses Official Over Passport Searches" (1992, p. 4A). In the wake of the Tailhook accusations of sexual abuse, the Secretary of the Navy and two admirals resigned ("Navy Secretary," 1992, p. 1A; "Investigation," 1992, p. 12A). In these examples, the suggestion is that the wrongful act will not recur because the person (allegedly) responsible for the wrongful act is no longer in a position to commit the offense and that appropriate punishment has occurred. Appropriate corrective action can help restore the face of a person guilty of wrong-doing.

These familiar examples demonstrate that the communicative act of repairing a damaged reputation is commonplace. Because blame occurs throughout human society and because face is important for virtually everyone, this phenomenon, a felt need to cleanse one's reputation with discourse, occurs throughout our lives, public and private. The ubiquity of this communicative phenomenon is one reason this topic merits scholarly attention. Cody and McLaughlin (1990) develop several other reasons for studying image restoration or accounts: to show how ordinary social actors understand their world through causal explanations; to examine how poorly handled predicaments can create conflict; to show that predicaments often involve rewards and punishments for participants; and to help actors maintain a positive self-image.

Various approaches are available for examining verbal self-defense, some developed in the rhetorical literature and some in sociology. Unfortunately, there is no complete analysis of this important and pervasive type of discourse. An examination of the literature reveals three key statements on image restoration through discourse, in the works of Burke, Ware and Linkugel, and Scott and Lyman. These are not, of course, the only works on this topic; others preceded or extended and applied their work. Nevertheless, these are clearly foundational writings in the area of image restoration discourse.

Kenneth Burke offers a more theoretical analysis of image restoration discourse than most treatments in the rhetorical literature. He uses the term "guilt" to represent an undesirable state of affairs that can be remedied through defensive discourse (other factors may create guilt, but attacks on our reputation would surely motivate rhetors to attempt to remove or reduce guilt). Burke explains that there are two fundamental processes for expunging guilt or restoring one's good reputation: victimage, scapegoating, or shifting the blame; and mortification or admitting wrong-doing and asking forgiveness (see, e.g., Burke, 1973). Rhetorical critics have applied Burke's analysis to public discourse (see, e.g., Brummett, 1981; or Foss, 1984).

The first systematic approach to rhetorical criticism of speeches of self-defense was developed by Rosenfield (1968). However, Ware and Linkugel's (1973) theory of apologia was much more widely used in rhetorical criticism. Drawing on the work of social psychologist Abelson (1959), they identify four factors or rhetorical strategies in rhetorical self-defense: denial, bolstering, differentiation, and transcendence. Ware and Linkugel suggest that these four strategies are combined in pairs to form four postures of defense. Again, rhetorical critics have applied Ware and Linkugel's theory of apologia to image restoration discourse (see, e.g., Katula, 1975; Kruse, 1981a; Short, 1987; or Vartabedian, 1985b).

Scott and Lyman's (1968) classic work on accounts, extending earlier work by Sykes and Matza (1957), offers a taxonomy for the provision of accounts for behavior subject to the criticism of others. Following Austin (1961), they distinguish between two general types of accounts. Excuses are accounts in which the accused admits that the act was wrong in some way, but does not accept full responsibility for that act. Justifications, on the other hand, accept responsibility for the act but reject the claim that it was a wrongful act. Later work in the tradition initiated by Lyman and Scott includes that of Schonbach (1980), Schlenker (1980), Tedeschi and Reiss (1981), and Semin and Manstead (1983).

Defensive utterances (justifications, excuses, apologies) are persuasive attempts to reshape another's beliefs, to change his or her belief that the act in question was wrongful, or to shift his or her attribution of responsibility for that act. This book explores this pervasive human discourse form. Chapter 2 begins this process by examining rhetorical scholarship on speeches of self-defense or *apologia*. Chapter 3 reviews work on image restoration and accounts. Based on these analyses, chapter 4 elaborates a general theory of image restoration. This theory is then illustrated through applications to defensive discourse in corporate and governmental affairs. Coke and Pepsi's struggle in the pages of trade publication *Nation's Restaurant News* is examined in chapter 5.

Chapter 6 examines Exxon's defensive rhetoric after the *Valdez* oil spill. Chapter 7 investigates Union Carbide's discourse concerning the Bhopal gas leak. Chapter 8 focuses on President Nixon's discourse defending his decision to invade Cambodia during the Vietnam War. Finally, chapter 9 discusses the implications of these and other analyses for the theory of image restoration.

Rhetorical Approaches to Image Restoration

This chapter, devoted to reviewing rhetorical approaches to image restoration, is divided into six sections. First, early, embryonic rhetorical criticism of image restoration discourse is reviewed. Then four systematic approaches to analysis of this genre of discourse are examined, one at a time: Rosenfield's analog, Ware and Linkugel's theory of *apologia*, Burke's theory of purification, and Ryan's *kategoria-apologia* approach. The sixth and final section discusses work that does not fit neatly into these categories. Although some studies of apologetic or image restoration criticism are undoubtedly overlooked, this review is designed to survey the research typically cited in the literature.

The underlying thesis of this chapter is twofold. First, current image restoration theory tends to be descriptive rather than prescriptive. That is, general treatments of image restoration tend to focus on identifying options rather than making recommendations concerning which options to use. Second, while there is a considerable body of rhetorical criticism that analyzes image restoration discourse, these approaches are largely independent of one another. Individual studies in this area, in the main, focus on explication of particular apologetic rhetorical artifacts rather than on contributing to a general understanding of image restoration discourse. Nevertheless, many interesting and useful essays investigate this recurrent form of discourse.

EARLY CRITICAL STUDIES OF SELF-DEFENSE DISCOURSE

Baskerville's (1952) analysis of Richard Nixon's "Checkers" speech as part of a symposium on campaign rhetoric is one of the earliest examples of rhetorical criticism of defensive discourse. In this essay Baskerville exposes weaknesses in Nixon's arguments. Nevertheless, he suggests that this speech was effective in large part because it created a favorable facade for the audience. McGuckin's (1968) more extensive analysis of this speech focuses on the values Nixon employed, arguing that this speech kept him as Eisenhower's running mate through successful identification with American values. Although McGuckin discusses an Aristotelian conception of ethos, neither McGuckin nor Baskerville clearly emphasizes image restoration.

Jackson's (1956) study of Clarence Darrow is another early rhetorical criticism of image restoration discourse. This is an example of a traditional (neo-Aristotelian) rhetorical criticism, describing the background and the outcome of the case and evaluating the effectiveness of Darrow's speech in self-defense against charges of bribing a jury. Jackson, following Maloney's (1955) general analysis, describes four features of Darrow's defense: providing historic background (Darrow alleged his trial was a result of his efforts to defend the poor and downtrodden), characterizing the prosecution as evil, using invective against the prosecution, and engaging in self-praise. These essays began to examine self-defensive rhetoric on a case-by-case basis, but as yet there was no theory to guide our understanding of this type of discourse. It is worth noting that as early as the mid-1950's it had been recognized in rhetorical criticism that attacking the opposition was a viable defensive strategy (Jackson, 1956).

ROSENFIELD'S ANALOG

The first theoretical advance in our understanding of image restoration discourse occurred when Rosenfield (1968) performed an analogic analysis of the "Checkers" speech by Nixon and a speech by Truman. The "Checkers" speech by Nixon has been a popular subject for rhetorical critics, having already been analyzed by Baskerville (1952). McGuckin's (1968) article on the "Checkers" speech appeared the same year as this piece by Rosenfield; and Ryan (1988b) would include a chapter on this speech in his book (see also Vartabedian, 1985a).

In this speech, Nixon defended against charges that he benefited from a campaign "slush" fund. Truman's speech responded to allegations that he had permitted a known Communist to remain in his administration. Rosenfield identified "four similarities in the two discourses which I take, at this time, to represent constants in the apologetic equation" (1968, p. 449). The four characteristics of apologetic discourse identified in Rosenfield's analog are: a brief, intense controversy; attacks on the opponent; a concentration of data in the middle third of the speech; and a recycling of arguments from recent speeches. While this theory is a useful beginning, the first factor describes the scene more than the discourse, and the third and fourth factors give us no idea what sorts of claims or rhetorical strategies are developed by the data lumped in the middle or by the recycled arguments. Furthermore, the second factor recognizes that attacks on one's opponents are another plausible strategy for dealing with criticism (as Jackson [1956] observed).

Butler (1972) extended Rosenfield's work to explain why Kennedy's Chappaquiddick address was unsuccessful. (However, Ling's [1970] prior analysis supports the opposite conclusion; furthermore, I challenged the evidence for her claim that this speech was unsuccessful [Benoit, 1988]; Kruse [1977] also questioned her conclusion.) Wilson's essay (1976) integrates Rosenfield's work (1968) with Ware and Linkugel's theory of *apologia* (1973). Despite these further applications, Rosenfield's theory fell into disuse, eclipsed by Ware and Linkugel's theory of *apologia*. Some time later, Campbell persuasively argued that it is unwise to attempt to develop a genre on the basis of an analog of but two instances (1983; see also Benoit, 1991b), undermining the logic of Rosenfield's conception of analogic criticism. Nevertheless, his analysis of these two defensive discourses occupies an important place in the development of our understanding of this recurrent form of rhetoric.

WARE AND LINKUGEL ON *APOLOGIA*

The next important advance in rhetorical criticism of image restoration discourse is the theory of *apologia*. After an initial study of a speech of self-defense by Sam Houston by one of the authors of this theory (Linkugel & Razak, 1969), Ware and Linkugel (1973) proposed the theory of *apologia*. Drawing on the work of social psychologist Abelson (1959), they identify four factors, or rhetorical strategies, in rhetorical self-defense. The first factor, denial, "consists of the simple disavowal by the speaker of any participation in, relationship to, or positive sentiment toward whatever it is that repels the audience" (p. 276). Simply put, the rhetor declares "I didn't do it!" If those accused of wrong-doing can disassociate themselves from the object of the audience's displeasure, then this strategy should help to restore the rhetors' image. Nixon's "Checkers" speech, in which he denied charges that he had benefited from a "slush fund," is offered as an example of this strategy. Ware and Linkugel include denial of bad intent (basically, claiming that the act was performed with good intentions) here as well.

Bolstering, the second factor, "is any rhetorical strategy which reinforces the existence of a fact, object, or relationship." In bolstering, "a speaker attempts to identify himself with something viewed favorably by the audience" (p. 277). In other words, bolstering is not aimed directly at the cause of the speaker's image problems (this strategy neither disassociates the rhetor from the undesirable action nor attempts to reduce that event's perceived unpleasantness). Rather, it attempts to counterbalance or offset the audience's displeasure by associating the speaker with a different object or action, something for which the audience has positive affect. The hope here is that the new positive perceptions of the rhetor will outweigh the negative ones from the undesirable act. Kennedy's Chappaquiddick speech is used to illustrate this strategy. In it, Ware and Linkugel explain, he repeatedly attempted to develop a positive relationship with the people of Massachusetts.

The third factor of self-defense is differentiation, an attempt at "separating some fact, sentiment, object, or relationship from some larger context in which the audience presently views that attribute" (p. 278). This factor takes the threat to the rhetor's image out of a negative context in the hopes that it is that negative context, and not the object itself, which arouses the audience's hostility. Kennedy's Chappaquiddick speech is also used to illustrate differentiation, as Ware and Linkugel suggest that the senator tried to distinguish his normal self from the person who narrowly avoided drowning.

Transcendence, the remaining factor of apology, "joins some fact, sentiment, object, or relationship with some larger context within which the audience does not presently view that attribute" (p. 280). In contrast to differentiation, which separates the object from an undesirable context, transcendence places that object into a larger or broader and more favorable context. Ware and Linkugel suggest that the latter functions to "move the audience away from the particulars of the charge at hand toward a more abstract, general view" (p. 280). They offer Clarence Darrow as an example of this rhetorical strategy. In the speech, "They Tried to Get Me," Darrow portrayed himself not as a criminal, but as the hero of the ordinary people.

In addition to developing the four factors of self-defense, Ware and Linkugel identify four potential postures or stances of self-defense. Speeches of self-defense, they declare, use either denial or bolstering, coupled with either differentiation or transcendence. This establishes four apologetic postures or stances of self-defense.

Absolutive:	Denial and Differentiation
Vindicative:	Denial and Transcendence
Explanative:	Bolstering and Differentiation
Justificative:	Bolstering and Transcendence

In a footnote, Ware and Linkugel acknowledge that an address may contain more than two of the four strategies (of denial, bolstering, differentiation, and transcendence). They "contend that the speeches of self-defense usually rely most heavily for their persuasive impact upon two of the factors" (1973, p. 282), although they do not elaborate the basis for this claim.

This theory of *apologia* has been a very popular approach for analyzing image restoration discourse. Kruse elaborated Ware and Linkugel's conceptualization of this theory. First, she employed Maslow's (1954) hierarchy to develop a typology of non-denial *apologia*, discussing survival, social, and self-actualized responses (1977). Second, drawing on Bitzer's (1968) analysis of the rhetorical situation, Kruse attempted to more clearly define the apologetic situation (1981b). She argued that apologetic discourse responds to attacks on character. This conception rather sharply limits use of the term "*apologia*," excluding it from situations in which (a) there is no formal attack and (b) the attack focuses on policy rather than character.

Rhetorical critics have applied the theory of *apologia* to a variety of defensive discourses. Harrell, Ware, and Linkugel (1975) employed it in an analysis of President Nixon's Watergate rhetoric. They argued that he adopted various postures (absolutive, justificative, and explanative) at various times and concluded that his defense was ineffective for several reasons: he never created the impression that he was in control; he attempted to provide structural justification for actions unacceptable to the public; and he lacked adequate support for his assertions.

Katula (1975) wrote that Nixon's resignation speech adopted the vindicative stance (denial and transcendence) and failed because it did not answer the questions which prompted the speech. Wilson (1976), on the other hand, argued that Nixon's speech employed bolstering and differentiation (an explanative posture) and was ineffective because it ignored the severity of his offense and was at odds with the reality he established. It would be interesting to see how these authors would react to the other's analysis, given their directly contradictory readings of this speech.

Post-Watergate *apologia* has also been examined with Ware and Linkugel's theory of *apologia*. Blair (1984) argued that Dean and Magruder used denial; Nixon and Stans used bolstering; Ehrlichman and Hunt employed bolstering and transcendence; Dean, Colson, Magruder, and McCord used differentiation; and Liddy employed transcendence. Kahl (1984) concluded that in *Blind Ambition* Dean relied on denial (of intent), while in *Lost Honor* he used differentiation and transcendence.

Vartabedian (1985a) applied *apologia* to two of Nixon's speeches, the "Checkers" speech and his 1973 Watergate speech. In the "Checkers" speech Nixon denied the charges that he had misused campaign funds (he denied that money went for personal use, he denied the fund was secret, and he denied that he had ever done favors for the contributors). He also used "differentiation/ counterattack" to distance himself from the democratic vice presidential candidate, John Sparkman (p. 56). Specifically, Nixon argued that the Democrats—unlike Nixon and Eisenhower—were associated with the ineffectual Truman administration: they were wealthy, they were soft on communism, and they were afraid to answer charges of improper conduct. None of these claims refer directly to the fund (the last concerns willingness to respond to charges), so they seem to function more as counterattack than attempts to differentiate Nixon's actions pertaining to the charges (but of course Ware and Linkugel's [1973] analysis does not include counterattack as a defensive option).

Vartabedian's (1985a) analysis of Nixon's Watergate speech reveals primary reliance on bolstering and differentiation. His efforts at bolstering were designed to "so strongly identify Nixon with his office that any wrongdoing by his subordinates was actually beyond his control" (p. 58). This sounds like shifting the blame, but again that is not one of Ware and Linkugel's categories.

Nixon differentiated the early reports (which concluded that no wrong-doing occurred) from later ones, to counter the suspicion that he had lied or been misinformed in earlier statements. He also distinguished between his direct management of his earlier campaign (in which he was not president) and his delegation of authority in this one (when he had the country to run).

Vartabedian (1985b) analyzed Nixon's 1969 Vietnam speech and his 1970 Cambodia address. Both discourses relied primarily on the strategies of bolstering and differentiation. Vartabedian concluded by arguing that Nixon had taken policy issues and transformed them into *apologia* (character issues), which is not consistent with dogma on the apologetic approach to image restoration (see especially Kruse, 1981b, who asserts that *apologia* deals with character but not policy issues, drawing a sharp distinction between these issues).

Hoover (1989) applied Ware and Linkugel's postures to former Tennessee Governor Ray Blanton's defensive discourse. She identified vindicative, absolutive, and a third posture, sometimes referred to as explanation/justification, but usually as explanative. This is somewhat confusing, because the two strategies she identified with it are bolstering and *transcendence*, which Ware and Linkugel define as a justificative posture (Ware and Linkugel define the explanative posture as employing bolstering and *differentiation*). Blanton's efforts were judged as unsuccessful, in part because he "appeared hypocritical and insincere" (p. 246) and because his values clashed with those of the audience.

Congressman George Hansen of Idaho attempted to restore his image after being convicted of filing false financial reports. Short (1987) reported that he denied the charges, attempted to transcend the charges by claiming the actions stemmed from his work on behalf of his constituents, bolstered his reputation, and attacked the IRS and other agencies (the last strategy, of course, extends Ware and Linkugel's categories).

Representative Wayne Hays was accused of having put Elizabeth Ray on the Congressional payroll, her "duties" consisting of being Hays's mistress. Morello (1979) reported that his speech to the House of Representatives primarily employed denial. However, Morello judged his speech to be largely unsuccessful, because the speech focused too much on a private concern (whether Hays had had a prior affair or was having a current mistress) and too little on the charge that most concerned the public (misuse of public funds for sex).

Gold (1978) applied Ware and Linkugel's theory to political discourse in general in the year 1976. She suggested that politicians continued to rely on denial (including denial of intent) and bolstering, but that they were generally "successful in defending themselves" (p. 516).

Ware and Linkugel's approach has also been used on sports rhetoric, by Kruse (1981a) and Nelson (1984). Kruse examined the occurrence of *apologia* in team sport. She concluded that sports figures employ the same strategies as other social and political actors. After disclosure of Billie Jean King's affair with her former secretary, defensive discourses by King and her husband, her peers, and the media were analyzed by Nelson. King and her husband used bolstering and differentiation (she was not an *active* lesbian). Her peers tended to use bolstering and transcendence (one's sex life should be private). The media employed bolstering and transcendence, as her peers had done. Nelson observed that King's non-denial *apologia* fit Kruse's survival motive (derived from Maslow's hierarchy). He also argued that this analysis showed that when more than one actor works together, they need not employ identical strategies, as long as the ones they use are not contradictory.

Burke (1988) applied *apologia* to discourse from a religious figure, analyzing Martin Luther King Jr.'s "Letter from Birmingham Jail." He argued that King's letter adopted the posture of explanation and that it used denial (King was not an outside agitator but had a right to be there), bolstering through identification, and transcendence (while we shouldn't break a just law, he opposed unjust laws).

Carlton (1983) argued that scaffold speeches constitute a distinct genre. Burkholder (1991) responded by arguing that it would be better to consider these discourses to be a species of *apologia*.

Furthermore, Ware and Linkugel's approach this perspective has been applied to corporate *apologia*. Lindsey and I examined Tylenol's response to the (first) poisonings, discussing three strategies: denial, bolstering, and differentiation (Benoit & Lindsey, 1987). These were appropriate and remarkably effective in restoring Tylenol's image, which several observers had wrongly concluded was irrevocably tarnished.

Finally, Downey (1993) reexamined speeches identified in the literature as apologetic, classifying them by time period, to investigate the evolution of this genre over time. She selected one of Ware and Linkugel's postures for each time period (classical: vindicative; medieval: justificative; modern: explanative; contemporary: absolutive; and post-1960: explanative). Although she discussed situational differences (for example, using the nature of the situation to explain the importance of religious references in medieval *apologia*) in the evolution of the practice of this genre, it is not clear the extent to which all examples of *apologia* from one time period do, or should be expected to, fall into a single one of Ware and Linkugel's postures. This analysis also appears to suggest that rhetors in each time period had but two principal strategic options (the two strategies constituting the dominant posture).

It also appears that Downey had to go beyond this theory in places. For example, she suggested that classical apologists enact vindication through denial and shifting the blame, although Ware and Linkugel do not discuss shifting the blame. She also found counterattack to be a recurring substantive feature, although this is also not one of Ware and Linkugel's strategies (she identified shifting the blame and invective as recurrent features of contemporary *apologia* as well). This essay provides a sweeping historic perspective to speeches of apology not possible with studies adopting a more limited purview.

Thus, many studies have applied—and in some cases extended—Ware and Linkugel's theory of *apologia*. Most analyses concern apologetic discourse from political figures, but sports, religious, and corporate applications have appeared. Together, they reveal the importance and utility of this theory to our understanding of image restoration discourse.

KENNETH BURKE ON PURIFICATION

A third approach to understanding image restoration discourse emerged from the writings of Kenneth Burke. Guilt is a primary motive in Burke's theory of dramatism. As Rueckert explains, "The two key moments of the drama are the negative and hierarchy, primarily because they are the principal guilt-producing factors" (1982, p. 131). The idea of "negative" permits human beings to create commandments against undesirable behavior that establish a hierarchy. Humans strive for perfection, to live within the hierarchy (actually, hierarchies) of society. However, because humans are imperfect, we inevitably break the commandments and experience guilt. As Burke (1970) puts it:

Here are the steps
In the Iron Law of History
That welds Order and Sacrifice:
Order leads to Guilt
(for who can keep commandments!)
Guilt needs Redemption
(for who would not be cleansed!)
Redemption needs a Redeemer
(which is to say, a Victim!)

Order
Through Guilt
to Victimage
(hence: Cult of the Kill) (Pp. 4–5)

Burke thus uses the term "guilt" to represent an undesirable state of affairs, an unpleasant feeling, which occurs when expectations concerning behavior are violated, as they inevitably are. While other factors may create guilt, attacks on our reputation—alleging that our behavior has been less than perfect, has violated important imperatives (commandments)—would surely motivate rhetors to attempt to remove or reduce guilt.

Burke explains that there are two fundamental processes for expunging guilt, or restoring one's good reputation: victimage, (scapegoating or shifting the blame) and mortification (admission of wrong-doing and request for forgiveness). (For useful summaries, see Foss, Foss, & Trapp [1985] or Rueckert [1982].) Victimage involves a transference or giving of the burden of guilt to a "vessel" other than the original accused (Burke, 1973, p. 39). The recipient of this guilt is the victim of this process, and, if the process is successful, guilt is shifted from the rhetor to the victim and the rhetor's reputation is cleansed. The alternative strategy, mortification, involves a sacrifice of self, an acceptance of wrong-doing. An apparently heartfelt confession and request for forgiveness may purge guilt and restore one's image. However, Burke explains that one's natural inclination is to use victimage (1970).

Ling's (1970) criticism of Kennedy's Chappaquiddick address, while focusing on the pentad (act, agent, agency, scene, and purpose), argued that Kennedy shifted the blame for the accident and Mary Jo Kopechne's death to the scene. Also focusing on the pentad, Kelley (1987) suggested that Representative George Hansen shifted the blame to his accuser, claiming that his felony fraud conviction was caused by a corrupt government. While he lost the election, the outcome was quite close, indicating that his rhetoric had been effective with many voters.

Brummett (1975) analyzed Nixon's Watergate speech of August, 1973. He suggested that one of Nixon's problems was that the more he stressed the context of his office, the more difficult it was to achieve identification. He also suggested that the president may have been better off with certain portions of the audience to have given an "expression of regret and apology" (p. 258), or, in Burke's terminology, to have engaged in mortification.

A Burkean rhetorical criticism of San Francisco Mayor Joseph Alioto's response to the "Zebra" murders was performed by Brummett (1980). He found that Burke's strategy of scapegoating or shifting the blame best characterized this discourse.

In an analysis of campaign discourse prior to the 1980 election, Brummett (1981) argued that Carter employed mortification (we are guilty of wasting energy), while Reagan used victimage (blaming the Carter administration for economic problems) and transcendence (arguing that consumption isn't bad, because it indicates progress). Brummett added a third possibility to Burke's strategies of purification (mortification and victimage): transcendence (see also Brummett, 1982). Brummett (1984) also discussed Burkean notions of comedy (victimage and mortification are tragic strategies).

Crable (1978) offered another analysis of the Watergate incident and the defensive discourse generated afterwards. He explained that to some extent Dean, Mitchell, and Ehrlichman all employed mortification, while Haldeman denied any wrong-doing, shifting the blame to Dean for all improprieties.

Representative Jim Wright resigned as Speaker of the House of Representatives. His discourse was judged as a failure by Collins and Clark (1992). He failed to establish his innocence and tried to blame the rest of Congress for misconduct.

Foss (1984) applied Burke to discourse designed to restore the image of Chrysler Corporation. While suggesting that Chrysler had to overcome guilt and tried to achieve redemption, Foss did not focus on the strategies identified by Burke for purging guilt. Instead, she described ten specific strategies for achieving redemption: portraying itself as a victim of changing times, association with the Japanese (quality), rebates (equated with mortification), dissociation from lower-quality products, comparison with other products, dissociation from the Japanese, emphasis of good gas mileage, endorsement by personalities, money-back guarantee, and American appeal. She concluded that initially this campaign had not been very successful, in part because of internal inconsistencies (e.g., comparisons with the Japanese) and the implication from the "bailout" that Chrysler was not a viable corporation.

Thus, several studies applied Burke to speeches designed for image restoration. This approach has also been extended (e.g., Brummett's [1981] addition of transcendence to victimage and mortification). Most research focuses on political rhetoric, but one study examines corporate rhetoric. Together, they demonstrate the pertinence and utility of this approach to understanding the reduction of guilt through discourse.

RYAN'S *KATEGORIA* AND *APOLOGIA*

The next stage in the development of our rhetorical understanding of image restoration discourse concerns Ryan's (1982) argument that one must carefully consider the defense (*apologia*) in light of the specific attack (*kategoria*):

> By checking each speech against the other, the critic is better able to distinguish the vital issues from the spurious ones, to evaluate the relative merits of both speakers' arguments, and to make an assessment of the relative failure or success of both speakers in terms of the final outcome of the speech set. Hence the critic cannot have a complete understanding of accusation or apology without treating them both. (P. 254)

He also explicitly expands the genre, especially from the conceptualization developed by Kruse (1981b), to include attacks on policy as well as character. However, he clearly sees a relationship between Ware and Linkugel's theory and his approach:

> In apology for policy, I contend that Cicero's four stases correspond to Ware and Linkugel's four postures in apology for character. The apologist for policy absolves himself of the fact (I did not do it), he explains the definition (I did not do what is alleged), he justifies the quality (I had laudable intentions), and he vindicates the jurisdiction (I appeal to a different audience or judge). (P. 257)

This approach is illustrated in its initial development by an analysis of the controversy between Pope Leo X and Martin Luther and later with an examination of the clash between Prime Minister Stanley Baldwin and King Edward VIII (Ryan, 1984; 1988a).

Ryan (1988a) also edited a book containing seventeen other illustrations of this approach. Most of these applications concern political figures, although a religious figure, a major corporation, a scientist, and a key trial are also represented here. This book has played an important role in developing Ryan's notion of the speech set. Because these studies were published in the same year, it is, of course, not possible to consider them chronologically. Instead, I will review the political discourses first and then the remaining speeches (ordering them alphabetically according to each essay's author in each category).

I analyzed Senator Edward Kennedy's Chappaquiddick speech (Benoit, 1988). The accusations against Kennedy included concerns about both his responsibility for the accident and his failure to report it promptly to the police. He attempted to shift the blame for the accident to situational features (the road, etc.). Kennedy also attempted to shift the blame for failing to report the accident to the trauma he suffered (exhaustion, a concussion). These strategies were effective in keeping his Senate seat, but probably were not sufficient to resurrect his presidential hopes.

Brock's (1988) analysis of President Gerald Ford's pardon of Nixon argued that his ultimate defense did not meet the standards Ford established upon assuming the presidency. First, the pardon was so unpopular that it kept the nation from getting on with other important business. Second, he failed to treat the American people or Congress as partners. Finally, Ford failed to distance himself from Nixon's Watergate difficulties.

Senator Robert LaFollette was attacked for his failure to support Wilson during World War I. Burgchardt (1988) explained that he (counter-) attacked his opponents. Then he used transcendence to move the issue away from himself as a victim of attacks by his opponents to the issue of free speech or constitutional rights. Although he ultimately prevailed (retaining his Senate seat after a vote to expel him failed and eventually restoring his reputation), Burgchardt concluded that "his effectiveness as an antiwar spokesman was severely curtailed" (p. 10).

President Truman relieved General Douglas MacArthur of duty, a highly unpopular decision. Evidence of MacArthur's insubordination was the subject of a news conference, but Truman's speech argued that MacArthur's policies would lead to war. MacArthur's defensive speech, delivered before a joint session of Congress, defended his policy and outlined actions he recommended (but Truman rejected). Discussing his language and delivery, Duffy wrote that MacArthur's speech was "animated in an auditory and visual drama that was less cerebral than emotional and moving" (1988, p. 92). In the final analysis, Truman's speech was probably more correct, but MacArthur's was more moving.

President Reagan's decision to visit and lay a wreath at a German military cemetery at Bitburg provoked a storm of controversy, especially when it was learned that it also contained the graves of SS troops. Friedenberg (1988) explained that Elie Wiesel, chair of the U.S. Holocaust Memorial Council, noted writer, and recipient of the 1986 Nobel Peace Prize (and a survivor of the Holocaust himself), suggested that this act would be interpreted by many as an act of homage to the German soldiers. This accusation was repeated during the ceremony in which the president presented Wiesel with a Congressional Gold Medal. At a press conference, Reagan erred by attempting to suggest that the German soldiers were victims like the Jewish people. This is simply not a persuasive comparison. However, in a speech after the visit, President Reagan argued more effectively that his actions should be taken as an attempt to achieve reconciliation (not homage), and he attempted to bolster his image by associating the United States (and himself) with a Jewish cause.

After legislation supported by President Franklin D. Roosevelt suffered several defeats in Congress (especially his "Court-packing" plan), he attacked several recalcitrant Democrats in the 1938 primaries, attempting to secure a more tractable Congress. He accused them of being too conservative, unwilling to try new solutions. Gravlee's (1988) essay analyzed responses by Senator George, Congressman O'Connor, and Senator Tydings. Senator George justified his voting decisions and bolstered his reputation by noting his support for selected New Deal legislation. Then he praised the president for past achievements while blaming presidential advisors and appointees. Congressman O'Connor bolstered his own image and attacked his accuser (specifically, an editorial used by the president in his attack on O'Connor). Finally, Senator Tydings bolstered himself and attacked his primary opponent. Senators George and Tydings won their primaries, while Congressman O'Connor lost. Gravlee suggested that the president might have been more effective if he had not given speeches in Georgia and

Maryland (against George and Tydings); press conferences might have appeared less extreme (which might explain why his accusation against Congressman O'Connor of New York appeared to be more successful). Furthermore, Roosevelt might have been better off if he had focused more on policy accusations (instead of character) and offered specific solutions.

Haapanen (1988) examined the verbal battle between Khrushchev and Eisenhower. After the Soviet Union shot down a U2 reconnaissance plane, Soviet Premier Nikita Khrushchev announced this in his opening speech to the Supreme Soviet. After a press release denied that the airplane had been spying, Khrushchev delivered the second part of his accusation, revealing that they had captured the pilot and thus had hard evidence to disprove the American lie. Eisenhower's response was to hold a press conference in which he admitted and accepted responsibility for the overflights, which he argued were justified on the basis of national security. This approach generally worked well for Americans and allies, but the incident and its handling may well have undermined the Paris Summit Conference.

Heisey (1988) studied President Ronald Reagan's apology in the Iran-Contra affair. The president was charged with trading arms for hostages, which is not only an accusation against policy, but, because he had vowed never to negotiate with hostage-takers, functioned to attack his character as well. Heisey's analysis examined numerous speeches and press conferences in which the president used denial, emphasized investigations, stressed his good intentions, attempted to refocus his audience's attention (away from the arms deal), and, after the Tower Commission Report revealed his involvement, he announced changes in personnel and procedures to correct the problem. Although his popularity dropped during the crisis, he eventually succeeded in putting this episode behind him.

Henry (1988) analyzed Senator John F. Kennedy's handling of the religious question during his presidential campaign. In Kennedy's Address to Newspaper Editors, he declared that he was not a "Catholic candidate for President," attacked the press for emphasizing religion more than other important issues, and bolstered his reputation by stressing his record. In his debate with Humphrey, he once again attacked accusers, declared that the Constitution says there shall be no religious test for president, and reinforced his image by stressing the separation of church and state. Finally, in his speech in Houston, he declared that he would not follow the dictates of the Catholic Church; he again attacked accusers by asserting that there were more important issues in the campaign than religion; and he shifted the focus from church-state separation to religious tolerance. Kennedy was successful in sweeping aside his opposition and securing the presidency.

General Hugh S. Johnson attacked Senator Huey Long and Father Charles Coughlin on behalf of President Franklin D. Roosevelt and his "New Deal." This attack and their defenses were analyzed by Huxman and Linkugel (1988). Long did attack the New Deal, but his speech primarily justified his Share the Wealth plan, and, after using transcendence to redefine policy accusations into character attacks, defended his character indirectly through discussion of his proposed policies. Father Coughlin offered a vituperative and inconsistent attack on Johnson. A point-by-point refutation (denial) of charges focused the audience's attention on those charges. Huxman and Linkugel concluded that Long's transcendental defense was more effective than Coughlin's refutative one.

Jensen (1988) analyzed Congresswoman Geraldine Ferraro's response to accusations about her finances and stance on abortion. In her *apologia* for finances, Ferraro supported her image by declaring that she would answer any question (she had nothing to hide) and by disclosing financial information. In her apology on abortion, she quoted John F. Kennedy's Houston speech and denied that she had claimed the Catholic Church's views on abortion weren't monolithic. Jensen suggested that Ferraro never had a reasonable opportunity to defend her image, because the press "virtually controlled the form and content of the debate" (p. 261).

Ryan provided an analysis of the clash between Prime Minister Stanley Baldwin and King Edward VIII (1988a; see also Ryan, 1984). The prime minister accused the king of wanting to marry a divorced commoner. Edward tried to justify his action on the basis of his love for Mrs. Simpson. This failed, because his subjects assumed that a king's duty to his country is his most important value.

Ryan (1988b) also analyzed Senator Richard Nixon's "Checkers" speech. Nixon engaged in bolstering as he mentioned his career in public service, including his role in the matter of Alger Hiss. He denied that the money had gone to him personally, he denied that it was a secret fund, and he denied providing political favors for contributors. He justified the fund as saving taxpayers' money, and he attacked his opponents. Although some were not persuaded, he was clearly successful in his bid to remain on Eisenhower's ticket as vice president.

President Richard Nixon's *apologia* on the Watergate scandal is analyzed by Smith (1988). Nixon's key strategies were denial and scapegoating, but neither were effective. Nixon's denials were untenable and ultimately furnished the substance of the charges against him along with the evidence substantiating them. Nixon attempted scapegoating with Haldeman and Ehrlichman, but this was ineffectual, because he tried to exonerate them while announcing their resignation. He also attempted scapegoating with Dean. This backfired, because Dean employed mortification, and Dean implicated Nixon as he admitted guilt.

Burke (1988) examined Martin Luther King Jr.'s "Letter from a Birmingham Jail" using Ware and Linkugel's approach. He reported that King adopted the posture of explanation, using denial (he was not an outsider: he had a legal and moral right to be there); bolstering (through identification); and transcendence (segregationists are correct that we shouldn't break the law, *but* these laws are unjust). In connection with his strategy of transcendence, he also counterattacked, arguing that Birmingham's laws were unjust: (1) only some were required to obey the laws; (2) the people denied the right to vote by law couldn't vote on that law; and (3) segregation laws denied the constitutional right of peaceful assembly. Burke concluded that this was an effective *apologia*.

Dionisopoulos and Vibbert (1988) looked at the controversy between CBS and Mobil Oil. CBS broadcast a report on excessive profits in the oil industry in which Mobil Oil figured prominently. Mobil denied charges of unethical bookkeeping and charged CBS with unfair reporting that didn't serve the public interest. CBS attempted to purify through denial. It refused to change its report, but it also declared that its report had not been an attack on Mobile, but on all of the oil industry. It distanced itself from the accusations by arguing that expert sources, not CBS, actually made the charges. CBS attempted to discredit Mobil by pointing out that it had refused to be interviewed (did it have something to hide?), and CBS declared that it refused to be intimidated.

Scientist J. Robert Oppenheimer was the subject of Holloway's chapter (1988). She found that he explained his early associations with Communists by suggesting that he was naive. Second, he denied that he had urged anyone to refrain from working on the H-bomb. Third, he bolstered his opposition to the project by referring to other prominent scientists who opposed it.

Finally, Lessl (1988) examined the Scopes trial. He revealed that both William Jennings Bryant and Clarence Darrow attempted to portray themselves as victims while attacking the other person. Neither adopted a pure role of defender, while each attempted to portray the other as aggressor.

These studies demonstrate the usefulness of Ryan's claim that it is important to examine the defense in light of the attack. While earlier work on speeches of self-defense did not deny this claim, no one advanced such a forceful claim and justification for it before Ryan's work. However, while these studies generally adopt his *kategoria-apologia* approach (some, rhetors like Ford and Edward Kennedy did not have single accusers), the authors did not uniformly follow his lead in embracing Ware and Linkugel.

OTHER IMAGE RESTORATION CRITICISM

Not surprisingly, several studies do not fall neatly into these categories, although they generally have points of intersection with the work already reviewed. I will mention examples of this work as it appeared over the years.

Dorgan (1972) analyzed rhetoric from Confederate veterans after the Civil War. He reported four recurrent themes: the Confederate cause was a glorious sacrifice; defeat is not a negative moral judgment; the defeat reflects divine will; and the defeat served a greater, long-term, good.

I analyzed Nixon's discourse in the Watergate scandal (Benoit, 1982), identifying a number of strategies that emerged as his defense developed over time (and shifted over time in some ways as the situation facing him altered): emphasizing investigation, shifting blame, refocusing attention, indicting his main accuser, emphasizing confidentiality, emphasizing his mandate, emphasizing cooperation, using executive privilege, and quoting from the transcripts. His defense was ineffective in part because he shifted the blame to his own handpicked subordinates, which meant that he was still ultimately responsible for Watergate.

Hahn and Gustainis (1987) identified recurrent arguments in defensive presidential rhetoric. These are grouped around three presidential myths: "(1) all problems are caused by outgroups, (2) our leaders are benevolent heroes who will lead us out of danger, and (3) the function of the citizen is to sacrifice and work hard to do the bidding of the leader" (p. 44). Their "topoi" are meant to be descriptive (rather than evaluative) and are illustrated with examples from several presidents.

Benson (1988) studied Johnson & Johnson's defensive strategies after the second *Tylenol* poisoning episode, concluding that it successfully used flexibility (tentative language, strategic ambiguity, trial balloons, portraying actions positively) and proaction (communicating frequently, using visible spokespersons, and portraying motives positively).

Reagan's rhetoric on the EPA (Environmental Protection Agency) Superfund controversy was analyzed by Rowland and Rademacher (1990). They reported that he effectively employed three main strategies: emphasizing his general commitment to positive values (here, the environment) rather than advocating specific (environmental) policies, blaming his subordinates, and taking action that was symbolic to end the crisis (nominating an impressive candidate, William Ruckelshaus). However, relatively similar strategies in his speech on Iran-Contra in response to the Tower Commission Report (stressing important values, blaming subordinates, and making appointments and changing procedures) were not as successful. His "passive style" was much less appropriate in important policy questions—like arms sales to Iran—than in details of EPA operation.

Using a preliminary version of the theory of image restoration discourse advanced here, Gullifor, Panici, and I analyzed Reagan's discourse on the Iran-Contra affair (Benoit, Gullifor, & Panici, 1991). Although his defense developed through several stages (in part as the situation changed), there were instances of denial, evasion of responsibility, minimization, mortification, and plans to correct the problem. He was most successful when he shifted from an overall stance of denial to one of mortification (for analyses of Reagan's discourse from non-rhetorical perspectives, see Abadi, 1990; or Snyder & Higgins, 1990).

Benoit and Brinson (1994) analyzed AT&T's image repair discourse following an interruption in its long-distance service in New York City during September 1991. After an unwise and unsuccessful attempt to shift the blame to lower-level workers, AT&T took out full page advertisements in the *New York Times*, the *Wall Street Journal*, and the *Washington Post*. This defensive discourse employed mortification, corrective action, and bolstering. The defense was appropriate and apparently successful in repairing its damaged image.

CONCLUSION

The literature on communication is replete with studies of image restoration discourse. The theories of image restoration are useful and insightful and provide a solid foundation for understanding image restoration discourse. Furthermore, we have numerous penetrating case studies of image restoration in the rhetorical criticism surveyed here. Most research tends to follow Ware and Linkugel, Burke, or Ryan, who, along with Rosenfield, have done the seminal work in this area.

This investigation of speeches of self-defense seems to share four common, although unstated, assumptions concerning image restoration discourse. First, these studies must assume that one's reputation is important. Why else would so many rhetors work so tenaciously to restore it when attacked? Second, this work assumes that when such attacks occur, verbal means of redress exist. Third, these attacks must be assumed to be sufficiently pervasive to require a theory of verbal self-defense. Finally, the literature on *apologia* seems to assume that a relatively limited number of defensive options are available to apologists. Table 2.1 lists the strategies described in the three typologies which dominate the rhetorical literature on image restoration.

As noted at the outset, this chapter provides the basis for two claims about the rhetorical study of image restoration discourse. First, this work is largely independent. For example, in 1956, Jackson's analysis of Clarence Darrow's discourse revealed the use of invective against his accuser. Similarly, Rosenfield's (1968) study of speeches by Truman and Nixon concluded that attacking one's accuser appears to be a constant feature of this genre (self-defense). However, Ware and Linkugel (1973), writing in the same field, failed to include this as an option. (While Kenneth Burke has published in *Quarterly Journal of Speech* and has been embraced warmly by many in the field, it is not clear that he is best characterized as belonging to the speech communication field.) While their work was noteworthy for drawing on work from conflict resolution (psychologist Robert Abelson), it cannot be viewed as exhaustive. Ware and Linkugel explain that their purpose is to "discover those *factors* which characterize the apologetic form" (1973, p. 274). Their characterization is valuable, but clearly incomplete. Nor does subsequent work (e.g., Wilson's [1976] attempt to integrate Rosenfield's approach with Ware and Linkugel's *apologia*, or Ryan's discussion of the relationship between Ware and Linkugel's

Table 2.1. Rhetorical Image Restoration Theories

Rosenfield	Ware & Linkugel	Burke
short, intense clash		
facts lumped in middle third		
recycled arguments		
attack accusers		
	denial	
	bolstering	
	differentiation	
	transcendence	
		victimage
		mortification

theory of *apologia* and his speech set analysis of *kategoria-apologia*) remedy this situation. The independence of this work is graphically demonstrated in table 2.1, in which there is no overlap between lists of image restoration options. An integrative analysis of rhetorical work on image restoration discourse is long overdue.

The second claim supported by this review is that the theories guiding this work are more descriptive than prescriptive. That is, Ware and Linkugel's theory of *apologia* and Burke's two means of purification present options available but do not offer advice about using these alternatives (nor does Rosenfield's list of four similarities suggest options or choices available to the rhetor). When should one use denial or bolstering, differentiation or transcendence? Burke suggests that rhetors are more inclined to use victimage than mortification, but does not address the question of the the relative effectiveness of these image restoration strategies. Hence, rhetorical theories of image restoration are descriptive rather than prescriptive. Of course, exploratory work is often descriptive in nature, but perhaps it is time to focus more on offering suggestions concerning when to use certain image restoration strategies.

Nor do the explanations offered by rhetorical critics necessarily help in this regard. For example, Harrell, Ware, and Linkugel (1975) suggest that Nixon's Watergate rhetoric failed, in part, because he did not create the impression that he was in control and because he lacked support for his claims. Wilson (1976) suggested that Nixon's resignation speech failed because it was not appropriate for the severity of the offense. According to Hoover (1989), Blanton's discourse was unsuccessful because he created the impression of insincerity and hypocrisy. Foss' s (1984) Burkean analysis of Chrysler's discourse suggested that internal inconsistencies and the negative image created (a company that needed a "bailout") undermined the effectiveness of this defense. None of these explanations relate to use of the theory of self-defense itself.

Of course, there is no question that the appearance of sincerity and a positive image (credibility), adequate support (evidence), and consistency are important factors in rhetorical discourse generally. When these factors seem to account for success or failure of a speech, then rhetorical critics must of course use them to understand the speech. However, my point is that in many instances, critical applications of image restoration theories do not seem to advance our knowledge of the specific genre (*apologia*) being studied. This is not meant as a negative commentary on any piece of rhetorical criticism, but as an assessment of the need for our study of image restoration discourse to go beyond describing options.

3   Accounts and Image Restoration

This chapter addresses theories of image restoration that deal with accounts and received their primary development in the social science literature. It discusses early work that established key assumptions, typologies of accounts, account phases, reproaches and accounts, usage of accounts, honoring (accepting) accounts, and accounts as a form of speech act. The most extensive section discusses typologies of accounts. It will become readily apparent that the lists of image restoration strategies developed in this literature are much more detailed than those in the rhetorical realm, although there is not as much application to public cases of image restoration found in the rhetorical criticism literature (see also reviews by Cody & McLaughlin, 1985, 1990; Morris, 1985).

EARLY ASSUMPTIONS

Heider (1944) discussed the assumptions that undergirded the analysis of accounts in discourse, recognizing that one's image or reputation is influenced by the quality of acts for which one is held responsible: "an act of low value, when attributed to the ego, will lower the ego level, and an act of high value will raise it" (p. 368). He realized that this provides a motivation for image management: "the tendency to raise the ego level will structure the causal limits in such a way that only good acts and not bad ones are attributed to the own person" (p. 369). Heider cited work by Claparede (1927) that distinguished between two options for dealing with problematic events: excuse (denying responsibility for the undesirable act) and imputation (blaming others for the negative act).

Early work by Dewey (1922, 1939) discussed motive, which was defined as an utterance that arose *after* an event to explain or account for it. As Mills (1940) explained, "When an agent vocalizes or imputes motives, he is not trying to *describe* his experienced social action. He is not merely stating 'reasons.' He is influencing others—and himself. Often he is finding new 'reasons' which will mediate action" (p. 909). Thus, "motives" were treated not in this literature as internal states that induce or guide behavior, but as utterances that explain or justify behavior after its occurrence.

Austin's (1961) essay attempted to call scholarly attention to "excuses." He argued that excuses arise "where someone is said to have done something which is bad, wrong, inept, unwelcome, or in some other of the numerous possible ways untoward. Thereupon he, or someone on his behalf, will try to defend his conduct or get him out of it." This is consistent with the previous work by Heider, Dewey, and Mills. Austin also suggested that we have two basic options, to "accept responsibility but deny that it was bad; in the other we admit that it was bad but don't accept full, if even any, responsibility" (p. 124). Later these two image restoration options came to be known as excuses and justifications, respectively.

In these works we see key assumptions of subsequent analyses of accounts in discourse. This form of utterance attempts to explain or justify our behavior against the unfavorable perceptions of others. These utterances may be called motives (a term that fell into disuse) or excuses, justifications, or rationalizations. Such statements come in two basic forms: denial of responsibility for the unpleasant act and reduction of the negative perceptions associated with the act. Scholars investigating this phenomenon developed extensive lists of accounting strategies, often grouped into excuses and justifications.

TYPOLOGIES OF ACCOUNTS

A number of lists of strategies for dealing with threats to one's reputation have been proposed in the literature. This section describes lists of accounts from Sykes and Matza, Scott and Lyman, Goffman, Schonbach, Schlenker, Tedeschi and Reiss, and Semin and Manstead. Each will be discussed in turn.

Sykes and Matza

The first typology of accounts, offered by Sykes and Matza (1957), was developed as a contribution toward understanding juvenile delinquency. Their analysis discussed five different "techniques of neutralization." Denial of responsibility includes unintentional or accidental acts. Denial of injury claims that no actual harm was done, even if the act is considered inappropriate: "Oh, you aren't really hurt!" Denial of victim can suggest that the injured party "deserved" it or that the victim is unknown. Harm done to the innocent may be viewed as worse than harm to the guilty. The accused may condemn his or her attackers, which tends to change "the subject of the conversation" (p. 668); that is, a counterattack may shift attention away from charges against you to your allegations against them. Finally, an appeal to higher loyalties justifies an action based on appeal to a different reference group; "You are being fired for the good of the company" exemplifies this defense. These strategies are listed in table 3.1. An operationalization of these techniques was developed subsequently by Rogers and Buffalo (1974).

Sykes and Matza's approach is somewhat unusual in that they argued that these strategies may precede and legitimize delinquent behavior, or "pre-empt" possible objections (see also the work by Hewitt & Stokes, 1975, and Bell, Zahn, & Hopper, 1984, on "disclaimers"). Most conceptualizations of accounts see them as utterances which occur after, rather than before, the offensive behavior. Other proposed terms for this sort of behavior include Hewitt and Hall's concept of quasi-theories (1973; see also Hall & Hewitt, 1970, Stokes & Hewitt, 1976, and Hopper & Morris, 1987, for discussions of aligning actions).

Scott and Lyman

One of the most influential approaches to the study of image restoration has been Scott and Lyman's (1968) analysis of accounts. Scott and Lyman defined an account as "a statement made by a social actor to explain unanticipated or untoward behavior" (p. 46) and distinguished between two general types of accounts, consistent with Austin's (1961) basic analysis. Scott and Lyman explain that "Excuses are accounts in which one admits that the act in question is bad, wrong, or inappropriate but denies full responsibility." Justifications, on the other hand, "are accounts in which one accepts responsibility for the act in question, but denies the pejorative quality associated with it" (p. 47). Each of these possibilities are subdivided further in Scott and Lyman's essay.

First, they identified four different types of excuses. Accidents provide excuses when we explain that unanticipated factors influenced our behavior. For example, "blaming one's lateness to work on the heaviness of traffic" is an example of an excuse based on accidents (1968, p. 48). An excuse takes the form of defeasibility when one lacks the knowledge ("No one told me the Xerox machine was out for repairs!") or the will (intoxication, mental illness) to successfully complete an action. They also suggested that this form of excuse could be equated with Sykes and Matza's technique of denial of responsibility. Biological drives may also serve as excuses (minors may be less able than adults to control their urges). The final type of excuse, scapegoating, alleges that one's undesirable behavior was a "response to the behavior or attitudes of another." An example might be the adolescent who spends a lot of time with "undesirable" persons (and getting into trouble with them) because his parents criticize or complain about his behavior whenever he is at home. This final form of excuse might be better labeled "provocation," given other uses of "scapegoating" that claim another person actually performed (as opposed to instigated) the offensive action.

Second, drawing on the work of Sykes and Matza (1957), Scott and Lyman proposed four types of justification: denial of injury, denial of victim, condemning the condemners, and appeal to loyalty. To these possibilities Scott and Lyman added sad tales (explaining or justifying current misbehavior on the basis of past difficulties) and self-fulfillment (explaining or justifying misbehavior as important to personal satisfaction). (See table 3.1 for a listing of these options. For other discussions of accounts, see also, e.g., Beach, 1990/1991; Buttny, 1985, 1993; Ditton, 1977; Harvey, Weber, & Orbuch, 1990; Morris & Hopper, 1980; Morris, White, & Iltis, 1994; Newell & Stutman, 1988; or Potter & Wetherel, 1987.)

Goffman

Goffman (1971) discussed what he termed remedial moves in conversation, extending his earlier work (1967). He identified five possible accounts as responses to a face-threatening event. First, the offender may issue a "traverse" or "rejoinder," denying that the offensive act actually occurred or that the offender committed it

(p. 109). Second, it is possible to admit that the act occurred (and that the actor was responsible) but redefine it as not offensive (similar to Scott and Lyman's strategy of justification). A third option is to admit that the act occurred (and that the actor was responsible for it) but to argue that the negative consequences were not reasonably foreseeable. The offender may also admit that the act occurred but claim reduced competence (similar to Scott and Lyman's notion of excuses). Finally, and, Goffman argues, least effectively, one may admit carelessness in performing the act or ignorance of the undesirable consequences of the act. Carelessness/ignorance is different from the third strategy, which argues that while the accused failed to see the consequences, no one could have been expected to foresee the outcome.

Goffman suggested another way to handle a problematic situation: an apology. He observed that while accounts have been widely discussed in the literature, apologies aren't extensively addressed, although "they are quite central" (1971, p. 113). An apology consists of a symbolic splitting of the self into two parts: the bad self, who committed the undesirable act, and the good self, who deplores that act. A complete apology has five elements: expression of regret, acknowledgment of expected behavior and sympathy for the reproach, repudiation of the behavior and the "self" committing it, promise to behave correctly in the future, and atonement and compensation.

Finally, Goffman (1971) discussed requests as remedial moves. Accounts and apologies typically appear after the wrongful behavior, although he acknowledged that it is possible for either to precede it. Requests, on the other hand, typically are found before (or at the beginning of) the event. Such an utterance "consists of asking license of a potentially offended person to engage in what could be considered a violation of his rights" (p. 114). Requests function to reduce the ill feeling that might be generated by untoward behavior. For example, before jostling another person in the press of a crowd, one might ask, "Do you mind if I try to squeeze past you?" Tracy (1990) also offers a useful discussion of facework (cf. Ting-Toomey, 1994). (See table 3.1.)

Schonbach

Around 1980, three separate essays offered updated analyses of Scott and Lyman's theory of accounts. A short essay by Schonbach diverged the most from Scott and Lyman's account (1980; see also

1987). He defined "failure event" to include "both deviant acts committed and obligations omitted" (p. 195). Acknowledging both Scott and Lyman's (1968) and Sykes and Matza's (1957) earlier taxonomies, Schonbach (1980) presented a new taxonomy based both on the previous literature and on accounts elicited from subjects who were asked to imagine themselves in a failure event (see table 3.1). The primary difference between Schonbach's and Scott and Lyman's systems is the addition of two major categories, coordinate with excuses and justifications, labeled concessions and refusals. Concessions include full or partial admission of guilt, expressions of regret, and offers of compensation (cf. Goffman's concept of apology). Refusals may deny that the failure event occurred, suggest that others are responsible, or suggest that the accuser has no right to attack. Schonbach also offered finer distinctions than made previously (e.g., Scott and Lyman offered "denial of victim" as a form of justification; Schonbach listed two variants of "role of victim": "justification of the damage with qualities of victim" and "justification of the damage with acts of victim") and additional subcategories (e.g., illness, addiction, drunkenness seem to be specific variants of Scott and Lyman's defeasibility [p. 146]).

Unfortunately, Schonbach (1980) did not illustrate all of the categories he proposed. For example, it is not clear what is meant by the refusal form "referral to other sources of information" (p. 197). Similarly, he did not discuss the reasons underlying some of his distinctions (e.g., why is it important or useful to have separate categories for *past* restitution or compensation and offers of *future* restitution or compensation?). However, he did offer a useful, if brief, analysis of accounts—especially his addition of concessions and refusals as possible responses to accusations (see also McLaughlin, Cody, & O'Hair, 1983, who propose that silence be added to Schonbach's analysis).

Schonbach (1990) extended his work on accounts. He reported the results of several studies and produced an extensive list of accounts. It consists of fourteen concessions, thirty-nine excuses, twenty-seven justifications, and forty-two refusals. (These categories are displayed in table 3.1.)

Schlenker

One modification of Scott and Lyman's theory of accounts was developed in an interesting book on impression management. Schlenker (1980) defined predicaments as "situations in which events have undesirable implications for the identity-relevant images actors have claimed or desire to claim in front of real or imagined audiences" (p. 137). The intensity of a predicament is directly related to its severity and the actor's apparent responsibility for it. Schlenker acknowledged that actors may attempt to avoid, conceal, or retreat from predicaments. However, at times actors must attempt to remedy these threatening predicaments.

Schlenker identified three forms of accounts, or "explanations of a predicament-creating event designed to minimize the apparent severity of the predicament" (p. 137, italics omitted): defenses of innocence, excuses, and justifications. Defenses of innocence attempt to demonstrate that the actor had nothing to do with the supposed untoward event: either the event never happened or, if it did, the actor was not responsible for it. The first form is like Schonbach's strategy of claiming that the failure event did not occur, and such defenses of innocence extend Scott and Lyman's typology.

The second major form of remedial move, excuses, attempts to minimize responsibility for the event. This can be attempted by claiming the consequences were not (or, better, could not have been) foreseen or claiming extenuating circumstances. Two variants of extenuating circumstances were mentioned by Schlenker: scapegoating, or arguing that others provoked the event (citing Scott and Lyman); and diffusion of responsibility or suggesting that one or more others were involved, reducing the responsibility attributable to any individual. This latter possibility is again an extension of Scott and Lyman's theory, but it can be found in Schonbach's work as well (participation of others in the failure event).

The third general form of account discussed by Schlenker, justifications, tries to mitigate the objectionable nature of the event. The actor may attempt to minimize the unpleasantness of the event directly, by comparison with others who are not punished (and possibly have done worse things), and by justification through higher goals. Direct minimization includes Scott and Lyman's notion of denial of victim, but also includes minimizing the negative consequences of the predicament. Comparison with others includes Scott and Lyman's tactic of condemnation of the condemners, but is broader in scope because it includes comparisons with others who aren't accusers as well. Finally, justification through higher goals extends Scott and Lyman's list. (These strategies are included in table 3.1.)

Tedeschi and Reiss

Tedeschi and Reiss (1981) offered another revision of Scott and Lyman's conception of accounts. Unlike Schonbach, they did not add additional general categories (like "concessions") to those of Scott and Lyman, but focused on excuses and justifications. They elaborated such categories as defeasibility. Scott and Lyman intend for this type of excuse to include such claims as "not fully informed," "misinformation," "intoxication," "lack of intent," and "failure to foresee the consequences" (1968, pp. 48–49), all of which appear as separate categories in Tedeschi and Reiss. However, in addition to these excuses mentioned but not given separate categories by Scott and Lyman, Tedeschi and Reiss also added new excuses, such as "distraction by other events," "lack of time for deliberation (e.g. crisis)," "drugs," "coercion by others," "hypnotized," and "brainwashed."

Tedeschi and Reiss also discussed justifications as responses to predicaments. Once again, they elaborated on Scott and Lyman's typology, offering, for example, six (new) specific types of "self-fulfillment." Similarly, Scott and Lyman listed "appeal to higher loyalties" as a form of justification, and Tedeschi and Reiss listed four different sorts of loyalties. They also added new justifications, such as several forms of appeal to higher authority (e.g., God, Satan, government), reputation building, appeal to norms of justice, and appeal to humanistic values. One interesting category is reputation building, which ironically attempts to restore a tarnished reputation by arguing that an act was done to enhance one's reputation. Oddly enough, Scott and Lyman's justification of "sad tales" does not appear to be included in this list. (This typology of accounting strategies is also included in table 3.1.)

Semin and Manstead

Semin and Manstead (1983) reviewed most of this literature (omitting only Schlenker's treatment) and offered a synthesis of these categories. Although they discussed Schonbach's system, they did not include either concessions or refusals. In other respects, this approach is the most complete discussion of accounts of those reviewed thus far. (Like the others, it is displayed in table 3.1.)

These approaches to image restoration can be broadly grouped into two sets of theories. One deals with exclusively with excuses and justifications (Sykes & Matza; Scott & Lyman; Tedeschi & Reiss;

and Semin & Manstead). The other group of theories includes, in addition to excuses and justifications, denial, refusals, or claims of innocence (Goffman; Schlenker; and Schonbach) and apologies (Goffman and Schonbach). (Tedeschi & Reiss include mistaken identity, a form of refusal, so an argument could be made for placing them in the second group.) This work has as its goal the development of detailed and extensive lists of image restoration strategies.

ACCOUNT PHASES

Although most of the work reviewed here focuses on creating typologies of strategic options for restoring face, other issues have been addressed as well. Goffman (1967) suggested that accounts passed through four moves: challenge, offering, acceptance, and thanks. Schonbach's (1980) analysis indicated that account episodes pass through four phases: the failure event, a reproach, the account, and an evaluation of the account. Cody and McLaughlin (1985) argued that accounting sequences consist of at least three basic moves: request for repair, remedy, and acknowledgment. Similarly, Buttny (1987) argued that account episodes involve three steps: problematic event, account, and evaluation. He argued that accounts do not necessarily reply to an (overt) reproach: "For instance, an offended person may pass from reproaching the offender, and allow the offender the opportunity to initiate the account" (p. 77), or the victim may not know of the offending act when the actor offers an account. (See also the discussion by Morris [1985].)

While these authors may not agree on whether it is the problematic event or a reproach (request for repair) concerning that event which constitutes the initial part of an accounting sequence, there is general agreement about this process. A person commits (or is believed to commit) an act that appears undesirable to another person or persons. Typically, this results in a reproach or request for a repair. Either the act (and assumptions about negative reactions to the act) or a reproach about the act provoke a response, the actor's account. This account is then evaluated by the person or persons to whom it was issued. Finally, the offending actor may offer thanks for acceptance of the account.

Schonbach (1990) reports an interesting series of studies organized around the phases of an account. In some studies, subjects are asked to role-play the reproach. In other research, subjects role-play the actor and provide either tape-recorded or written accounts in response to a challenge or reproach provided by the researcher. Finally, in a third group of studies, subjects are asked to role-play the other, evaluating accounts provided by the researcher.

REPROACHES AND ACCOUNTS

Schonbach and Kleibaumhuter (1990) asked subjects to imagine that they had been involved in a problematic situation (a child they had been baby-sitting drank some cleaning fluid and required medical treatment) and to respond to one of three remarks from the child's parents: a neutral question, a reproach derogating their self-esteem, or a reproach derogating their sense of control. Either form of reproach elicited fewer concessions and more justifications and refusals than the neutral question (no difference occurred in the number of excuses offered). This finding is generally replicated in the studies described in Schonbach (1990). Similarly, McLaughlin, Cody, & O'Hair (1983) reported that mitigating reproaches tended to elicit mitigating accounts, while aggravating reproaches were more likely to elicit aggravating accounts. However, McLaughlin, Cody, and Rosenstein (1983) found that use of concession, excuse, and justification were not associated with particular reproaches. Refusal to account was likely when the other used rebuke, request for account, and superiority. Thus, while the evidence is mixed, the use of reproaches (or aggravating reproaches) may elicit fewer conciliatory responses.

USAGE OF ACCOUNTS

This section will discuss production of accounts in response to face-threatening predicaments. First, general treatments of account production will be reviewed. This will be followed by a discussion of severity of offense and extent of blame on account production. Finally, research on when people use false accounts will be reviewed.

Gonzales, Pederson, Manning, and Wetter (1990) report that in a contrived accident, subjects produced more mitigating (concessions, excuses) than aggravating (justifications, refusals) responses. When asked to provide responses in hypothetical situations, Gonzales, Manning, and Haugen (1992) report that concessions were produced most often, followed by excuses, justifications, and refusals (in that order). Garrett, Bradford, Meyers, and Becker (1989) report that telephone interviews with managers of corporations that had been boycotted produced accounts in these proportions: justifications: 72 percent, denial: 13 percent, excuse: 11 percent, and concession: 5 percent. Schonbach's (1990) role playing studies indicate that subjects provided situational constraints (both as excuses and justifications), expressed regret (generally, regret for their role in the offense, and regret for consequences to the victim), and, least frequently, expressions of concern with pleas for pardons. McLaughlin, Cody, & O'Hair (1983) added a fifth general type of account (silence) to Schonbach's four major types of accounts (concessions, excuses, justifications, and refusals). They asked subjects to recall accounts they had provided to others in the past. Excuses were the most frequently reported form of account (63 percent), followed by concessions (30 percent), justifications (22 percent), refusals (13 percent), and silence (5 percent). Thus, concessions and excuses tend to be produced more often than justifications and denials. Refusals (denials) are generally the least likely response to predicaments in this research.

Several relevant studies have been conducted under the rubric of the effects of embarrassment. Modigliani (1971) reports that self-reported embarrassment correlates positively with coded facework (utterances apparently intended to improve the subject's image). Metts and Cupach (1989) asked subjects to recall an embarrassing predicament and to report their response to it. Avoidance (e.g., pretending not to be bothered) was used more often than expected by chance; aggression (physically or verbally attacking others present) was used less often than chance; and there was no difference in the reported frequencies of remediation, humor, excuse, escape (physically leaving the scene), apology, and justification. Similarly, Cupach and Metts (1992) found avoidance and humor to be the most commonly recalled strategies for dealing with embarrassment, and aggression and apology plus (in this study categories were developed for utterances with multiple components) occurred least often (see also Cupach & Metts, 1990). Thus, when people feel embarrassed, they are likely to produce face-saving utterances. They often avoid the embarrassment or make light of it. Other accounting strategies (e.g., remediation, excuse, justification, apology) also occur, although less frequently.

Physical or verbal aggression is the least likely response to embarrassment. (See also work by Sharkey and Stafford [1990].)

Schlenker and Darby (1981) report that subjects were likely to offer more complex and fewer perfunctory apologies as the severity of the offense increased. McLaughlin, Cody, and O'Hair (1983) found that when the offense was serious, concession was a likely response. Concessions were more likely to occur when the apologist felt guilty; refusal and silence were more likely when the actor felt little or no guilt. Gonzales, Manning, and Haugen (1992) found that accounts contained more different elements when blameworthiness was high than low. However, McLaughlin, Cody, and Rosenstein (1983) found that use of concession, excuse, and justification was not associated with type of reproach (refusal to account was likely when the other used rebuke, request for account, and superiority). Thus, severity of the offense and apparent responsibility of the actor influence account production, although type of reproach does not seem to have an impact.

Weiner, Amirkhan, Folkes, and Verette (1987) asked subjects to recall situations in which they breached an expectation (late for appointment, failed to attend a party, failed to perform expected action). They were instructed to report two such situations, one in which they gave a true account and one in which they lied about the failure event (and when they lied, they were asked to reveal the actual reason). Recalled accounts were grouped into seven categories: transportation, work/school, other commitment, ailment, negligence, preference ("I decided I didn't want to go"), and miscellaneous. They found that the most frequent (actual) reasons that prompted lies were preference and negligence.

This research suggests that people prefer to provide excuses and concessions (rather than justifications, refusals, or silence) for their alleged misdeeds. This has been demonstrated with contrived accidents, hypothetical situations, and recalled behavior. The research on embarrassment suggests that, when possible, people prefer to pretend the predicament simply hadn't occurred (or wasn't very bad). Severity of harm and apparent responsibility for that harm have been found to influence production of accounts. Finally, when their personal preference or negligence is responsible for the predicament, people are more likely to offer false excuses than when other factors were responsible for the failure event.

HONORING ACCOUNTS

Several essays have addressed the question of when an account is likely to be accepted or honored. This section examines predictions from Scott and Lyman about effectiveness of accounts. This is followed by a discussion of the effects of account form on its acceptability. Then the role of apparent severity of offense and perceived responsibility of the actor on effectiveness of accounts is examined. Finally, an alternative to accounts is discussed.

Scott and Lyman (1968) suggest that an account will not be honored if it is considered to be either illegitimate or unreasonable. They explain that accounts are considered illegitimate when the undesirable behavior is more significant than the account or when the account concerns a motive not acceptable to the audience. Accounts are unreasonable when they do not reflect ordinary social knowledge of reasonable behavior and expectations.

One aspect of legitimacy of the claim is that the account must outweigh the offense. Evidence consistent with this notion is reported by Gonzales, Manning, and Haugen (1992), who found that participants predicted that their accounts would be less likely to be accepted when the consequences of their act were severe than mild. Blumstein et al. (1974) indicate that an account was more likely to be honored when the violation was minor than when it was serious. Similarly, Schwartz, Kane, Joseph, and Tedeschi (1978) report that negative evaluations and ratings of deserved punishment were directly related to severity of harm. While no direct test of the precise prediction has been conducted (the account is *more significant* than the offense), research suggests that accounts are more likely to be accepted when the offense is mild than severe.

The second component of legitimacy concerns the acceptability of a motive to the audience. Morris and Coursey (1989) indicate that three variables influenced managers' acceptance of employee accounts: the employee's reputation, the account's plausibility, and evidence that confirms or contradicts the account. However, Riordan, Marlin, and Kellogg (1983) report that believability (whether subjects believed the account was the actual reason for the act) was not related to attributions of responsibility and perceptions of the act. Thus, there are conflicting results on the relationship of an account's plausibility or believability on its effectiveness.

Accounts are also predicted to be unacceptable when they are inconsistent with ordinary social knowledge. Riordan, Marlin, and Kellogg (1983) indicate that normativeness (the degree subjects believed others would offer a similar account in similar situations) did affect attributions of responsibility and perceptions of the act. Thus, some of Scott and Lyman's predictions concerning honoring of accounts have received research support.

Research has also investigated the effects on honoring of the form of an account. One study found denials (and excuses) to be effective accounts. Riordan, Marlin, and Gidwani (1988) asked psychologists to respond to hypothetical accounts for unethical practices. Denials decreased perceived wrongness of the act, followed by excuses, while justifications were evaluated as most wrongful. Denials produced more positive evaluations of the actor than excuses or justifications. McClearey (1983), operating from Ware and Linkugel's theory of *apologia* (see Chapter 2), reported that denials were better than bolstering at improving image and in decreasing blameworthiness. Finally, researchers who offered justifications were believed more likely to repeat the act than those who gave excuses (see also Riordan & Marlin, 1987).

McLaughlin, Cody, and French (1990) investigated perceptions of those charged with two common forms of traffic offenses, running a red light and speeding. Those who used logical proofs (apparently denial with supporting evidence) were thought less likely to have been penalized and less likely to have been responsible or to have intentionally broken the law. Challenge (a combination of denial without evidence and questioning the officer) was relatively ineffective for the red light case. Excuses produced high levels of blameworthiness in both cases, while justification did so in the speeding case.

Other research suggests that excuses are an effective response to a face threat. McLaughlin, Cody, and Rosenstein (1983) found that excuse was associated with honoring and that justification and concession were associated with retreat (partial honoring, withdrawal, or excuse-making by the victim on behalf of the offender). However, their regression analysis also found that justification was associated with rejection/reinstatement. Shields (1979) found that those who used excuses were seen as more remorseful than actors who used either justifications or confessions. Gonzales (1992) reports that concessions and excuses created more positive impressions of the offender than refusals.

However, other research suggests that justification can be a useful strategy for image restoration. Hale (1987) reported that justifications created a more favorable impression of the actor than excuses, concessions, or apologies. Schonbach (1990) reports that excuses were rated as less justifiable than justifications.

Other research did not show overall superiority for either excuse or justification. Riordan, Marlin, and Kellogg (1983) report that actors who used excuses were thought to have less foreknowledge of negative consequences of the act and less intent to produce those consequences (than justifications). They found that justifications did reduce the perceived wrongness of the act compared with excuses. Shields (1979) found that there were no differences in perceived responsibility for excuses, justifications, and confessions.

Research tends to show that the presence of an apology can create a more favorable impression of the actor (than no apology). When a boy expressed remorse for tripping a girl, he was viewed as less aggressive, less intentional, less likely to repeat the act, and less deserving of punishment than when he expressed pleasure (Schwartz, Kane, Joseph, & Tedeschi, 1978). Similarly, Ohbuchi, Kameda, and Agarie (1989) found that victims have more favorable impressions of actors, and were less aggressive toward them, when the actor apologized for causing an injury than when there was no apology. A second study using hypothetical situations also found that subjects believed a victim would have more favorable impressions when the actor apologized than when there was no apology. Darby and Schlenker (1982), working with children, found that apologies reduced unfavorable consequences for the apologist. More developed apologies (with attempts to compensate the victim) reduced blame, increased forgiveness, and increased liking more than less developed ones. Holtgraves (1989) found that hearers ordered accounts from most to least satisfying in this fashion: full-blown apology (apology, remorse, promise not to repeat offense, request for forgiveness, and request to provide compensation), regret plus excuse, apology, regret, excuse, regret plus justification, justification. Furthermore, Blumstein et al. (1974) found that an actor's account was more likely to be accepted if it expressed repentance and if the actor was thought unlikely to commit the offense again. Thus, there is consistent support for the effectiveness of apologies in managing threats to face (one exception is Hale, 1987).

Several studies address the effects of severity of the harm on an account's effectiveness. As mentioned earlier, Blumstein et al. (1974) and Gonzales, Manning, and Haugen (1992) found that an account is more likely to be honored when the severity of the offense is less than when it is greater. Rothman and Gandossy (1982), on the other hand, report that the harm of the crime influences the probation officer's sentencing recommendation more than the actor's relative role in the crime. So, research on the effects of perceived wrongness of the act tends to suggest that severity is inversely related to account effectiveness, although perceived responsibility appears important as well.

Blumstein et al. (1974) found that an account was more likely to be honored when the actor was not completely responsible for the offense. Gonzales, Manning, and Haugen (1992) report that participants thought their account would be most likely to be accepted by another when the act was accidental, least likely to be accepted when the act was intentional, with negligent acts moderately likely to be accepted. Similarly, Kane, Joseph, and Tedeschi (1977) found that actors perceived to have more choice in committing a criminal act were perceived less favorably, held more responsible, believed to be more likely to commit the offense again, and believed to deserve harsher punishment than actors perceived to have no choice. Recall that Rothman and Gandossy (1982) found that offensiveness was more influential than apparent responsibility. Still, in general, apparent responsibility for the wrongful act influences the effectiveness of accounts for that act.

Particular accounts (e.g., specific excuses) vary in effectiveness. For example, Kane, Joseph, and Tedeschi (1977) found that differences in the nature of the excuse determined the excuse's effectiveness. Those who committed criminal acts because of threats to their families were seen more positively, as less responsible, and less deserving of punishment than those who committed crimes because of threats to themselves. Drawing on the literature on attribution theory, Weiner, Amirkhan, Folkes, and Verette (1987) revealed that when asked to evaluate potential accounts, subjects reported that preference ("I decided I didn't want to do it") and negligence were more likely to create anger than accounts based on transportation, work/school responsibility, other commitments, or ailments. They suggest that accounts are more likely to be accepted when they are external, uncontrollable, and unintentional than internal, controllable, and intentional. Furthermore, Hale (1987) found that accounts perceived to be of higher quality (which she defined as accounts which represented "sensitivity to not only the instrumental but the identity and interpersonal dynamics of the encounter," p. 117) were more effective, regardless of the form of the account.

Finally, Mehrabian (1967) contrasted apology with another strategy for restoring face, redefinition of the situation. For example, when a person is late for an appointment, the actor can apologize for being late or thank the other person for waiting without apologizing (which assumes that the other was willing to wait). In ambiguous situations, both strategies were effective. However, when the situation was not ambiguous, apologies were preferred.

Thus, two of Scott and Lyman's three predictions on honoring accounts were confirmed: severity of offense is inversely related to effectiveness, and normativeness plays a role in the acceptability of excuses. There are conflicting results on the effects of the plausibility of accounts on honoring. Results on form were disparate. Only apology is generally found to be an effective form of account. Accounts are more likely to be accepted when the offensive act is less severe and the actor less responsible for that act. There is variance in the effectiveness of particular forms of accounts. Finally, when the situation is ambiguous, the actor may be able to redefine the situation so as to avoid threat to face (although apologies work in ambiguous and unambiguous situations).

Effectiveness of accounts has generally been found to vary inversely with severity of the offense and actor's perceived responsibility. Given that a threat to face must involve both a wrongful deed and a responsible actor, these findings are readily understandable. The fact that accounts should follow social norms should not be surprising. The finding that it is possible to redefine an ambiguous situation so as to lessen its threat to face is also reasonable. Finally, because apologies attend to the needs of the injured party and show the actor as concerned and remorseful, it is sensible to find that apologies are an effective form of account.

Why would there be such conflicting results on the effectiveness of the various forms of account? Several reasons can explain this muddle. First, this research employs multiple methods. Most studies (Blumstein et al., 1974; Holtgraves, 1989; McLaughlin, Cody, & French, 1990; Riordan, Marlin, & Gidwani, 1988; Riordan, Marlin, & Kellogg, 1983; Schwartz, Kane, Joseph, & Tedeschi, 1978; Schonbach, 1990; Shields, 1979) had subjects react to a hypothetical scenario and evaluate provided accounts, which assumes that they will be successful in taking the perspective of the offended party. Gonzales, Manning, and Haugen (1992) asked subjects (as offenders) to speculate about others' reactions to their accounts. Rothman and Gandossy (1982) use defendants' stories and probation officers' sentencing recommendations. Gonzales (1992) and Ohbuchi, Kameda, and Agarie (1989) inflicted harm on subjects (the latter also used a hypothetical situation in their second study). Morris and Coursey (1989) interviewed managers concerning reactions to employees' accounts. Those who are actually injured by another person might react differently from third parties. Given differences between actors and observers found in other research (see, e.g., Farr & Anderson, 1983; Jones & Nisbett, 1971; Street, Mulac, & Wiemann, 1988), it should not be surprising that different results might arise from such different designs.

Second, multiple dependent variables are assessed in this research. Some studies (Blumstein et al., 1974; Holtgraves, 1989) assessed whether subjects considered the accounts to be acceptable or satisfying, a global assessment. Similarly, other research assessed the subjects' affect for the offender (Gonzales, 1992; Hale, 1987; Ohbuchi, Kameda, & Agarie, 1989; Riordan, Marlin, & Gidwani, 1988; Shields, 1979; Schwartz, Kane, Joseph, & Tedeschi, 1978). Other research investigated the effect of accounts on perceived wrongness of the act (Blumstein et al., 1974; Riordan, Marlin, & Gidwani, 1988; Riordan, Marlin, & Kellogg, 1983; Rothman & Gandossy, 1982) and on the actor's apparent responsibility for the act (Blumstein et al., 1974; Gonzales, Manning, & Haugen, 1992; Kane, Joseph, & Tedeschi, 1977; McClearey, 1983; McLaughlin, Cody, & French, 1990; Riordan, Marlin, & Gidwani, 1988; Riordan, Marlin, & Kellogg, 1983; Shields, 1979; Schwartz, Kane, Joseph, & Tedeschi, 1978). Nor can these factors be considered equivalent, for Riordan, Marlin, and Kellogg (1983) found that the account form best at reducing apparent wrongness—justification—increased perceived responsibility (and the form which reduced responsibility—excuses—increased wrongness).

Third, as Holtgraves (1989) observes in explaining the difference between his results and Hale's (1987), operationalizations of the types of accounts vary widely. In these examples, Holtgraves's form of justification was denying harm, while Hale's justification was appeal to higher loyalties. Several of the general forms (especially excuse and justification, unquestionably the two most common general account forms) have varieties which vary in the extent to which they restore face. If one study uses quite different forms of excuse and justification from another study, dissimilar results seem possible if not likely.

Fourth, research indicates that specific instances of account forms (e.g., threat to family versus threat to self) vary in effectiveness. It seems possible that a researcher could accidentally have used, for example, a strong justification but an implausible excuse (or vice versa). This could account for conflicting results.

Finally, what appears to be an effective account in one situation (experimental scenario) might not seem to be a good choice in another. For example, if the scenario suggests (or declares) that an injury *has* occurred, denial (refusal) would not seem to be a good response. However, if the description of the scenario is unclear about whether the injurious act occurred, denial/refusal might be evaluated positively. For example, if the subjects are convinced that the actors did commit the offense, denial/refusal is unlikely to restore their reputation (indeed, they appear to be liars as well as perpetrators of the original offense). However, if the subjects are uncertain of the actors' responsibility, plausible denials could easily restore their reputations. Similarly, in McLaughlin, Cody, and French's (1990) study of traffic offenders, denial was more effective when it included logical proofs than a challenge of the officer. Thus, it is not clear that the results should be assumed to be directly comparable throughout these diverse studies.

ACCOUNTS AS SPEECH ACTS

As suggested earlier, Austin (1961) contributed to our understanding of accounts through his "plea for [studying] excuses." However, his writing in the area of speech acts (1962; see also Searle, 1969) also prompted a line of work on accounts as speech acts. For example, Fraser outlined four assumptions made about the person who offers an apology: the speaker believes an act occurred prior to the apology, the speaker thinks the act offended the listener, the speaker thinks he or she is responsible for that act at least in part, and the speaker feels remorse for the act (1981; see also Coulmas, 1981; and Edmondson, 1981). Fraser also described a variety of strategies for expressing an apology. A more extensive discussion of accounts as speech acts was presented by Owen (1983). Abadi (1990) presented a model of the speech act of apology, which is briefly applied to Prime Minister (of Japan) Takeshita's resignation speech and a speech by President Reagan on the Iran-Contra affair. While this work on accounts as speech acts is an important contribution to our understanding of this particular speech act, it is not primarily designed to describe strategic options available to the person who finds it necessary to repair a reputation. Rather, it focuses on developing a framework for determining when a particular utterance should be seen as an apology or on developing the assumptions and requirements for the "happy" performance of this act.

CONCLUSION

The work on accounts and image restoration shares certain key assumptions. People are seen as concerned with face or image: we generally want others to view us and our behavior favorably. Therefore, human beings are often motivated to offer accounts, or explanations, of our behavior to others. This phenomenon is likely to occur when we believe others will hold us responsible for behavior which we believe they perceive as undesirable. It is assumed that there are a limited number of options for rehabilitating one's reputation and that it is useful to identify those potential image restoration strategies. Many writers have tried to develop and improve lists of accounting behaviors, and table 3.1 depicts these efforts.

Much of this research has focused on developing detailed typologies of image restoration strategies, although there has been some experimental research in this area. Most theorists discuss two forms of accounts: excuses, which attempt to lessen or eliminate the actor's responsibility for the negatively perceived act, and justifications, which attempt to convince the audience that the act is not bad (or not as bad) as they initially believed. Some theorists also suggest that the apologist may protest innocence. The most complete description of excuses and justifications was developed by Schonbach (1990), with Semin and Manstead (1983) a close second.

Five stages of a complete account sequence have been identified (although writers do not discuss all five together): the offense; a challenge, reproach, or request for remedy by the injured party; the account, remedy, or offer; an evaluation of the account; and thanks or acceptance of the account.

People are more likely to use excuses and concessions (rather than justifications, refusals, or silence) as accounts. Research on embarrassment suggests that people prefer to ignore the predicament (or pretend it wasn't very serious). Severity of harm and apparent responsibility influence production of accounts. Finally, when their personal preference or negligence is responsible for the predicament, people are more likely to offer false accounts than when other factors are responsible for the failure event.

Two of Scott and Lyman's (1968) predictions have received empirical support: severity of offense is indirectly related to effectiveness, and normativeness influences the acceptability of excuses. There are conflicting results on the plausibility of accounts on honoring. Results on the effect of account form on effectiveness were mixed. The most consistent results supported the effectiveness of apologies. Severity of and responsibility for the wrongful act inversely related to account effectiveness. Particular instances of account forms vary in effectiveness. Furthermore, when the situation is ambiguous, the actor may be able to redefine the situation so as to avoid threat to face. People are more likely to lie in an account when personal preference or negligence was responsible for the offense than transportation, commitments, or illness. Finally, accounts have been analyzed as speech acts. Clearly, there are diverse approaches to understanding image restoration behavior in the literature on accounts.

Table 3.1. Theories of Accounts

Sykes and Matza (1957)

  denial of responsibility
  denial of injury
  denial of victim
  condemnation of condemners
  appeal to higher loyalties

Scott and Lyman (1968)

Excuses
  accidents
  defeasibility
  biological drives
  scapegoating

Justifications
  denial of injury
  denial of victim
  condemnation of condemners
  appeal to higher loyalties
  sad tales
  self-fulfillment

Table 3.1. Continued

Goffman (1971)

account
  denial
    that act occurred
    that accused committed it
  redefine act as not offensive
  consequences not foreseeable
  reduced competence
  carelessness or ignorance
apology
request

Schonbach (1980, pp. 196–97)

Concessions
  explicit acknowledgment of guilt
    full concession
    partial concession
  explicit abstention from excuse or justification
  express regret
    concerning own responsibility for event
    concerning consequences of event
  restitution or compensation
    appeal to past restitution or compensation
    offer of restitution or compensation

Excuses
  own human shortcomings
    insufficient knowledge or skill
    will impairment
  reason for appeal to own shortcomings
    biological factors (e.g., arousal)
    illness, addiction, drunkenness
    negative past
    provocation by others
    duress
    loyalties
    specifics of situation
  own effort and care
  shortcomings and misdeeds of others
    shortcomings and misdeeds of accuser
  participation of other persons in failure event
  participation of accuser in failure event

Justifications
  denial of damage
  minimization of damage
    in view of circumstances which demanded event
    positive consequences of event
  role of victim
    justification of damage with qualities of victim
    justification of damage with acts of victim
  right of self-fulfillment
    right of self-fulfillment in light of own negative past
  loyalties
  positive intentions
  shortcomings or misdeeds of other persons
    shortcomings or misdeeds of accuser

Refusals
  claiming failure event did not occur
  explicit refusal of confession of guilt
  application of guilt to other persons
    application of guilt to accuser
  denial of right of reproach
    on the basis of identity or role in relation to accuser
    on the basis of negative qualities or deeds of accuser
  referral to other sources of information
  evasions or mystifications

Schonbach (1990, pp. 188–95)*

Concessions
  Peripheral
    willingness to report on event
    acknowledge negative aspects of failure event
    acknowledge other's right or reason to question or reproach
  Admission of responsibility, guilt, mistake, shame, embarrassment
    partial admission of some responsibility
    full admission
    admission of responsibility with excuse or justification
    admission of shame or embarrassment
  Expressions of regret
    in general
    concerning own role
    for consequences of failure event to victims
    for inability to provide restitution or compensation

---

*Slightly modified for summary here; e.g., in one case a heading was supplied, consistent with the nature of the rest of the table.

Table 3.1. Continued

Announcement of restitutions/compensation
Formal offer of apology or request for pardon
Other concessions

Excuses
Pleas for mitigation in judgment, based on claims of impairment of
    capacity and/or volition
    capacity/volition from unspecified cause
    fatigue/exhaustion
    alcohol/drugs
    physical illness
    momentary affective or mental state
    mental illness
    lack of training/experience
    admission that one doesn't know what to say
(Claims of impairment due to external factors)
    claims of impairment due to situational constraints (including
    unforeseeability)
    claims of impairment due to time pressure
    claims of restriction of action from loyalties, norms, values, or stan-
    dards
Claims of impairment due to powerful agents (e.g., restriction of infor-
    mation or threatened punishment)
Claims of impairment due to provocation
    by accuser
    by victim
    by other persons
Pleas for mitigation in judgment, based on arguments other than
    impairment claims
Appeal to participation of other co-actors in the failure event as frames
    of reference for mild judgments
    accuser
    victim
    others
Appeal to limitations, negative traits or misdeeds of other persons as
    frame of reference for mild judgments
    accuser
    victim
    others
Plea for mitigation in judgment on the basis of assertions about actor's
    self, past or present
    underprivileged past
    good record in past
    present identity, role, or status

actor's role in failure event
conviction of the legitimacy of the failure event
good intentions (or lack of bad intentions)
effort and care
restitutions or compensations
learning experience of failure event
Plea for mitigation in judgment on the basis of assertions about characteristics of the future event
minimization of failure aspects
denial of damage
minimization of damage
positive consequences or side effects of failure event
Expressions of hope and concern
express hope for understanding, pardon, mercy and continuation of good relationship with victim
express concern for victim regarding damage from failure event
Other excuses

Justifications
situational constraints fully/partly legitimizing action
time pressure fully/partly legitimizing action
appeal to loyalties to norms, values, or standards
appeal to loyalties to specific persons
claims of obedience to or pressure from powerful agents
Claims of full or partial legitimacy in view of provocations by various agents
accuser
victim
others
Claims of full or partial legitimacy in view of participants of other agents in the failure event
accuser
victim
others
Claims of full or partial legitimacy of own behaviour in view of limitations, negative traits, or misdeeds of other persons
accuser
victim
others
Appeals to the right of self-fulfillment
underprivileged past
good record in past
present identity, role, or status
other arguments or without supporting arguments
Claims of full or partial legitimacy on the basis of assertions about actor's role in the failure event

Table 3.1. Continued

    conviction of the legitimacy of failure event

    good intentions (or lack of bad intentions)

    effort and care in connection with failure event

    restitutions/compensations

Claims of full or partial legitimacy on the basis of assertions about characteristics of failure event

    minimization of failure aspects of event

    denial of damage

    minimization of damage

    positive consequences or side effects of failure event

Other justifications

Refusals

    Refutation of allegation of a failure event or of actor's involvement in such an event

        denial of occurrence of failure event

        denial of involvement in failure event

        denial of opponent's right or reason to question/reproach (without supporting argument)

        refusal to concede guilt or responsibility for occurrence of failure event

        refusal to accept responsibility for solution (restitution or compensation)

        refusal to accept future task assignment related to failure event

        refutation of specific reproach or argument

    Unrestricted attribution of responsibility for the failure event to other persons

        accuser

        victim

        others

    Evasions and mystifications

        deferral of account

        referral of accuser to another source of information

        irrelevant talk

        silence

        other evasions or mystifications

    (Denial of the right to question or reproach in view of characteristics of the failure event)

        in light of unforeseeability or unpreventability of failure event due to situational constraints

        because of temporal constraints of failure event

        because of loyalties to higher norms, values, or standards

        because of loyalties to specific persons

        because of pressure from powerful agents

Denial of the right to question or reproach in view of provocations by various agents
accuser
victim
others

Denial of the right to question or reproach in view of participation by other persons as co-actors in the failure event
accuser
victim
others

Denial of the right to question or reproach in view of limitations, negative traits or misdeeds of other persons
accuser
victim
others

Denial of the right to question or reproach based on self-relevant comments
underprivileged past
good record in past
own identity, role, or status
right to self-fulfillment

Refutation of the right to question or reproach on the basis of assertions about actor's role in connection with the failure event
conviction of legitimacy of failure event
good intentions
effort and care in connection with failure event
restitutions/compensations

Refutation of the right to question or reproach on the basis of assertions about characteristics of the failure event
minimization of failure event
denial of damage
minimization of damage
positive consequences of side effects

Other refusals

Schlenker (1980, pp. 138–48)

Defenses of innocence
nonoccurrence
noncausation

Excuses
unforeseen consequences
extenuating circumstances
scapegoating
diffusion of responsibility

Table 3.1. Continued

Justifications
    direct minimization
    comparison
    higher goals

Tedeschi and Reiss (1981, p. 282)

Excuses
    lack of intention or assertion that effects were not planned
    accident
    failure to foresee consequences (plea of ignorance)
    effects unforseeable
    lack of information
    poor judgment
    distraction by other events
    misrepresentation of events by others
    mistake
    lack of time for deliberation (e.g., crisis)
    inadvertency
    mistook identity of target person
    lack of capacity (e.g., infancy, mental retardation)
    lack of volition or assertion of lack of bodily control
    physical causes
        drugs
        alcohol
        physical illness (e.g., fainting spell, temporary paralysis, etc.)
        exhaustion
    psychological causes
        insanity or mental illness
        overpowering or uncontrollable emotions (e.g., fear, anger, jealousy)
        coercion by others
        hypnotized
        brainwashed
        somnambulism
        lack of authority
        denial of agency
        mistaken identity (I didn't do it)
        amnesia and/or fugue state

Justifications (p. 288)
    appeal to higher authority
        God, Satan, spirits commanded
        Government official commanded
        high status/prestige person commanded

organizational rules stipulated
appeal to ideology
  nationalism/patriotism
  for the revolution
  to protect society or mankind
  to promote the religion or sect
  against oppression
appeal to norms of self-defense
  self-defense
  reciprocity
  revenge on associate of provoker
  clan/gang wars
  guilt by association
reputation building
  protection from coercion
  credibility maintenance
  machismo
appeal to loyalties
  friend
  long-standing understanding/relationship
  gang/group
  peer group, sex, race, etc.
appeal to norms of justice
  derogation of victim
  equity, equality, and social welfare norms
  law and order
effects misrepresented
  no harm done (no victim)
  benefits outweigh harms
social comparisons
  condemn the condemners
  scapegoating
appeal to humanistic values
  love
  peace
  truth
  beauty
self-fulfillment
  psychological health
  catharsis of pent-up emotions
  personal growth
  exerting individuality
  mind expansion and self-actualization
  conscience or ego-ideal

Table 3.1. Continued

Semin and Manstead (1983, pp. 91–92)

Excuses
    denial of intent
      accident
    unforeseen consequences, due to
      lack of knowledge
      lack of skill or ability
      lack of effort or motivation
      environmental conditions
      identity of target person mistaken
    denial of volition
      temporary (e.g., fatigue, drugs, illness, arousal)
      semi-permanent (e.g., paralysis, blindness, deafness)
    psychological causes originating in
      self (e.g., insanity, overpowering emotion)
      others (e.g., coercion, hypnotism, brainwashing)
      lack of authority
    denial of agency
      mistaken identity
      amnesia
      joint production
    appeal to mitigating circumstances
      scapegoating [provocation]
      sad tales
Justifications
    claim that effect has been misrepresented
      denial of injury
      minimization of injury (consequence only trivially harmful)
    appeal to principle of retribution
      reciprocity (victim deserved injury because of actions)
      derogation (victim deserved injury because of qualities)
    social comparison
      (others do worse things but go unpunished)
    appeal to higher authority
      powerful person(s) commanded
      higher status person(s) commanded
      institutional rules stipulated
    self-fulfillment
      self-maintenance (catharsis, psychological or physical health)
      self-development (personal growth, mind expansion)
      conscience (dictated)
    appeal to principle of utilitarianism
      law and order

self-defense
benefits outweighed harms
appeal to values
   political (e.g., democracy, socialism, nationalism)
   moral (e.g., loyalty, freedom, justice, equality)
   religious (e.g., charity, love, faith in deity)
appeal to need for facework
   face maintenance
   reputation building

4   A Theory of Image Restoration

This chapter develops a theory of image restoration discourse. First, the key assumptions that undergird this theory are described. Then, an integrated typology of image restoration strategies, drawing heavily on the literature reviewed in chapters 2 and 3, is developed. Finally, the relationship of this theory to other approaches to understanding image restoration discourse is explored. This chapter thus lays the groundwork for the application chapters to follow.

ASSUMPTIONS OF THIS THEORY

Two key assumptions provide the foundation for this theory of image restoration strategies. First, communication is best conceptualized as a goal-directed activity. Second, maintaining a positive reputation is one of the central goals of communication. Each of these assumptions will be discussed separately in this section.

Communication is a Goal-Directed Activity

The first assumption made by this theory is that communication is a goal-directed activity. One of the earliest and clearest indications of this assumption can be found in Aristotle's *Rhetoric*. In the fourth century B.C. Aristotle distinguished three genres of oratory based on the goal of the speaker.

> Rhetoric has three distinct ends in view, one for each of its three kinds. The political orator aims at establishing the expediency of the harmfulness of a proposed course of action . . . Parties in a law-case aim at establishing the justice or injustice of some

63

action. . . . Those who praise or attack a man aim at proving him
worthy of honour or the reverse (1954, 1358b21-28).

Each of the three genres Aristotle describes is directly tied to the
speaker's goal: political rhetoric concerns proving whether a policy should be adopted; judicial rhetoric decides questions of justice
or injustice; and epideictic rhetoric argues that a person is worthy
of praise or blame. In fact, in this description the goal is the key
defining feature that constitutes the genre.

More recently, Kenneth Burke, whose theory of rhetoric as symbolic action has been extremely influential in recent years, declares
that an act "can be called an act in the full sense of the term only if
it involves a purpose" (1968, p. 446). Elsewhere, Burke declares that
a passage from Milton "is clearly rhetorical. It occurs in a work written with a definite audience in mind, and for a definite purpose"
(1969, p. 4). This is not to suggest that Burke considers specific, conscious purpose to be the central defining characteristic of rhetoric.
However, even as he attempts to extend the purview of rhetoric
he seems to want to exclude "aimless utterances" "we also seek to
develop our subject beyond the traditional bounds of rhetoric.
There is an intermediate area of expression that is not wholly deliberate, yet not wholly unconscious. It lies midway between aimless
utterance and speech directly purposive" (p. xiii). Hence, for Burke,
rhetoric is purposeful—either directly or indirectly purposive.

Fisher (1970) is another theorist who recognizes the importance of goals or purpose in discourse, when he asserts that there
are four central "motives, or kinds of rhetorical situations" (p.
132). He identifies these as affirmation, which creates an image;
reaffirmation, which revitalizes one; purification, which reforms
an image; and subversion, which attacks an image. Thus Fisher
construes rhetoric as a goal-directed activity and interestingly
defines its purposes in relationship to images.

In fact, with few exceptions, most rhetorical theorists have
considered rhetoric to be the art of persuasion, a declaration typically carrying with it the assumption that rhetorical discourse is
purposeful (see, e.g., Arnold & Frandsen, 1984; Bitzer, 1968;
Booth, 1974; Bowers & Bradac, 1984; Miller, 1984; Richards, 1936;
Rowland, 1982; or Scott, 1980). Thus, much of the literature of
rhetorical theory, in general, assumes that rhetoric is a goal-
directed, purposeful, or intentional activity.

The assumption that communication is goal-directed can also
be found in the literature on communication theory (see, e.g., Hal-

liday, 1973). Clark and Clark, for example, declare that "speaking is fundamentally an instrumental act" (1977, p. 223). Several scholars have asserted that all messages have content and relational dimensions (see, e.g., Reusch & Bateson, 1951; Watzlawik, Beavin, & Jackson, 1967). Closely related to this claim is the idea that communication can be motivated by a limited set of intents, purposes, or goals. One fairly popular typology of communication purposes is advanced by Clark and Delia (1979), who indicate that there are three:

> issues or objectives explicitly or implicitly present for overt or tacit negotiation in every communicative transaction: (1) overtly instrumental objectives, in which a response is required from one's listener(s) related to a specific obstacle or problem defining the task of the communicative situation, (2) interpersonal objectives, involving the establishment or maintenance of a relationship with the other(s), and (3) identity objectives, in which there is management of the communicative situation to the end of presenting a desired self image for the speaker and maintaining a particular sense of self for the other(s). (P. 200)

The key point here is that the view of communication as goal-directed, while perhaps not universal, pervades writing in our field, transcending particular contexts of interpersonal communication or rhetorical theory. Craig even declares that "a practical discipline of communication in which the concept of goal would not be central is difficult to imagine; and the pragmatic language of goal, decision, and consequence is in fact the common coin of the discipline of speech communication that has emerged in the United States in this century" (1986 p. 257). Hence, it is appropriate to construe communication and rhetoric to be goal-driven activities.

Any assumption as broad as this one is likely to require qualifications, and this one is no exception. First, communicators may well have multiple goals that are not completely compatible. In such circumstances, behavior that functions to further one goal may well mean that other goals remain partially or completely unmet. It is even possible that utterances intended to further one goal may harm attainment of another. However, I contend that people try to achieve the goals that seem most important to them at the time they act, or to achieve the best mix of the goals that appears possible (considering the perceived costs of the behavior enacted in pursuit of the goals, and the importance of those goals to the actors).

Second, at times a person's goals, motives, or purposes are vague, ill-formed, or unclear. Nevertheless, to the extent a person's goals are clear, he or she will try to behave in ways that help to accomplish them. Furthermore, even when a communicator has a clear conception of a particular goal, that does not necessarily mean that he or she is aware of (and/or is willing or able to use) the most effective means for achieving that goal. However, to the extent a particular goal is salient to a communicator, he or she will pursue that goal by enacting the behavior that the communicator believes is likely to achieve that goal and has tolerable costs.

Third, I do not claim that people devote the same amount of attention to each and every communicative encounter, micromanaging all utterances and all characteristics of an utterance, constantly identifying goals and unceasingly planning behavior to accomplish them. Some behavior is automatic rather than controlled (see, e.g., Kellermann, 1992; Schneider & Shiffrin, 1977; Shiffrin & Schneider, 1977; or Hample, 1992). In situations that are particularly important to us, however, we do plan aspects of our utterances carefully. In other situations, we devote as much cognitive effort to producing goal-directed discourse as seems reasonable and necessary to us.

Finally, even when an individual's goals are relatively clear, it may be difficult for others (e.g., critics) to identify a communicator's goal(s). Of course, multiple goals (including "hidden agendas") complicate matters for critics. Similarly, if a person's goals are unclear to that person, it should be difficult for a critic to identify them. Another problem in identifying communicators' goals arises because people sometimes attempt to deceive or mislead others about their goals. Furthermore, certain artifacts (e.g., television shows, films, artwork) may not have readily identifiable persuasive goals, purposes, or intents for the critic to discover. Despite these reservations, communication generally is best understood as an intentional activity. Communicators attempt to devise utterances that they believe will best achieve the goals that are most salient to them when they communicate.

Von Wright's idea of the practical syllogism is a useful way to view communication. He explains the relationship between goals and action in this way:

A intends to bring about *p*.
A considers that he cannot bring about *p* unless he does *a*.
Therefore, *A* sets himself to do *a*.

A scheme of this kind is sometimes called a *practical inference* (or syllogism). (1971, p. 96)

Thus, when people have goals or desires (that they believe communication can help accomplish), they present the messages that they think will be instrumental in obtaining their goals. Of course, if there is more than one means of accomplishing a goal, they will choose the utterance that (they believe) maximizes the likelihood of success, or the utterance that (they believe) has the fewest costs, or the utterance that (they believe) also facilitates another goal. Furthermore, if people believe more than one utterance is required to accomplish their goal, they will offer several messages. They must believe the utterance is one they are capable of performing, that it is likely to help accomplish their goal, and that it does not have unreasonable costs. When these circumstances obtain, then speaker *A* will say utterance *a* in an attempt to accomplish goal *p* (see von Wright's chapter III, "Intentionality and Teleological Explanation," pp. 83–131).

Thus, communication is best conceptualized as an instrumental activity. Communicative acts are intended to attain goals important to the communicators who perform them. These utterances are ones which the communicators believe will help accomplish (with reasonable cost) goals that are salient to the actor at the time they are made.

Maintaining a Favorable Reputation is a Key Goal of Communication

The second key assumption of this theory of image restoration is that maintaining a favorable impression is an important goal in interaction. The need for discourse designed to restore our reputation arises because, as human beings, we inevitably engage in behavior that makes us vulnerable to attack. First, our world possesses limited resources: there is only so much money, time, office space, computer time, workers, and so forth. When the distribution of these scarce resources fails to satisfy a person's desires, dissatisfaction occurs. It is rarely possible to satisfy everyone, so these complaints naturally tend to recur. Second, events beyond our control can prevent us from meeting our obligations. Faulty alarm clocks can make us late, important mail may not reach us, or our computer system may go down when a critical report is due. Third, people are human, and so we make mistakes—some honestly, others because of self-interests. People accidentally lose things borrowed from others, they forget to attend meetings, individuals overcharge their clients. Alcohol, drugs, or even lack of sleep may cloud our judgment and impair our performance. Finally, and possibly most importantly, we often differ over goals. Conflict over goals or ends often creates dissension These four elements—limited resources, external events, human error, and conflicting goals—combine to insure that actual or perceived wrong-doing is a recurring feature of human behavior.

What are the consequences of such inevitable untoward behavior? Semin and Manstead report that when "breaches of conduct" occur, "actors assume that they have projected a negative image of themselves, even if the breach is an unintentional one" (1983, p. 38; see also 1981, 1982; Manstead & Semin, 1981; Semin, 1981, 1982). Furthermore, they indicate that "the threat of potential negative imputations to the self, in the shape of anticipated negative dispositional inferences that an observer may make, increases with the degree of blame and responsibility that can be inferred from the act" (1983, p. 38; see also Manstead & Semin, 1981; Semin, 1981). Thus, human beings worry that others will think less of them when apparent misdeeds occur, and this threat to their image is thought to increase as their responsibility increases. This is clearly related to Burke's notion of guilt, discussed in chapter 2, and embarrassment, addressed in chapter 3. These "negative imputations toward the self" arise from introspection.

However, exacerbating this tendency to feel guilty ourselves, others are often quick to criticize us when this kind of misbehavior occurs. They may complain about what we said or did, about things we didn't say or do, or even about the *manner* in which we did or said something. McLaughlin, Cody, and Rosenstein (1983) identified four types of reproaches or utterances that provoke accounts or apologies: expressing surprise or disgust, suggesting that the person being reproached is morally or intellectually inferior, requesting an account, and rebuking another person. It seems clear that a variety of possible reproaches or complaints can assail reputation or face. The importance of persuasive attacks has been recognized by Ryan (1982), who argues for the importance of considering *kategoria* for a complete understanding of *apologia*. While less work has been conducted on attacks than defense, there is some useful work in this area (see, e.g., Alberts, 1988, 1989; Morris, 1988; Pomerantz, 1978; and Vangelisti, Daly, & Rudnick, 1991).

Thus, our vulnerability to criticism leads to (internal) guilt and (external) threats to our face, both of which motivate a reaction from the actor. What happens when we believe that negatively perceived events threaten our reputation? Goffman explains that "When a face has been threatened, face-work must be done" (1967, p. 27). Notice also that Clark and Delia (1979), discussed above, identify the identity objective as a key goal in communication, and Fisher (1970) suggests that one of the basic motives of rhetoric is purification of an image. Why is face or image so important that persuasive attacks motivate defensive responses?

First, face or reputation is a crucial commodity because it contributes to a healthy self-image. Snyder, Higgins, and Stucky explain that "Achieving and maintaining a positive self-image have been postulated as important motivational variables throughout the history of psychology" (1983, p. 29; see also Schonbach, 1990). This is true because problematic events (threats to face) have a variety of undesirable consequences, as Schlenker explains:

> The more severe a predicament is, the greater the negative repercussions for an actor. The actor should experience greater internal distress such as anxiety and guilt, receive greater negative sanctions from audiences, and produce greater damage to his or her identity—thereby adversely affecting relationships with the audience. (1980, p. 131)

Thus, the literature concerning communication and interaction assumes that a person's face, image, reputation, or perceived character is extremely important.

A second reason why image or reputation is important concerns its role in the influence process. For example, in the *Antidosis*, Isocrates makes it clear that he considers the speaker's *ethos*, or prior reputation, to be important to the effectiveness of discourse:

> The man who wishes to persuade people will not be negligent as to the matter of character; no, on the contrary, he will apply himself above all to establish a most honourable name among his fellow-citizens; for who does not know that words carry a greater conviction when spoken by men of good repute than when spoken by men who live under a cloud, and that the argument which

is made by a man's life is of more weight than that which is furnished by words? (P. 278)

In fact, Isocrates goes so far as to argue that a rhetor's prior reputation is a more important factor in persuasion than arguments and evidence:

> probabilities and proofs and all forms of persuasion support only the points in a case to which they are severally applied, whereas an honourable reputation not only lends greater persuasiveness to the words of the man who possesses it, but adds greater luster to his deeds, and is, therefore, more zealously to be sought after by men of intelligence than anything else in the world. (P. 280)

Thus the assumption that *ethos*, credibility, or reputation is important pervades the rhetorical literature. Aristotle, for example, writes that "We believe good men more fully and more readily than others; this is true generally whatever the question is, and absolutely where exact certainty is impossible and opinions divided" (1954, 1356a6–8). Thus, for classical rhetoricians Isocrates and Aristotle, ethos is extremely important in persuasion. Similarly, attitude change theory and research also support the importance of credibility in facilitating persuasiveness (see, e.g., Andersen & Clevenger, 1963; Benoit, 1991a; Littlejohn, 1971). Therefore, one important goal of discourse is to establish and maintain a positive image or reputation.

Because one's face, image, or reputation is so important, Brown and Levinson (1978) observe that "people can be expected to defend their faces if threatened" (p. 66). Empirical evidence confirms the claim that perceived embarrassment is positively correlated with amount of facework (Modigliani, 1971). Therefore, when our reputation is threatened, we feel compelled to offer explanations, defenses, justifications, rationalizations, apologies, or excuses for our behavior. Because blame and criticism or complaints occur throughout human society and because face is important for virtually everyone, this phenomenon, a felt need to cleanse one's reputation through discourse, occurs in all our lives, public and private.

If we consider some of the examples related in chapter 1, we can see how they illustrate the assumption that communication is directed toward the goal of image restoration. When Woody Allen was accused of child molestation, he denied the charges. This utterance does not seem designed to bolster his professional career or to further a business deal. It seems quite straightforwardly intended to restore a damaged reputation. If his denial is accepted by its intended audience, his image should be restored. Coach Paul Westhead was fired after a dismal season with the Denver Nuggets. His response was to blame his players' lack of abilities. This reply seems to be concerned with correcting the impression that he was a poor coach. If his audience accepts this explanation of the team's losing season, that record should not be counted as evidence of Westhead's incompetence, and his reputation should be restored. When President Bush was criticized for issuing pardons in the Iran-Contra affair, he attacked his accusers for making "stupid" and "frivolous" charges. Again, this utterance seems designed to save (or restore) face. If his intended audience accepted his claims that the charges are stupid and frivolous, then his reputation should not suffer damage from them.

IMAGE RESTORATION DISCOURSE

This theory of image restoration assumes that communication is, in general, a goal-directed activity. It focuses on one particular goal in discourse: restoring or protecting one's reputation. We must keep in mind that this is not the only goal, or necessarily the most important goal, for a specific actor in a given situation. However, it is one of the central goals in communication. The approaches to understanding verbal attempts designed to restore sullied reputations reviewed in chapters 2 and 3 seem to share these assumptions concerning the importance of reputation or face, its susceptibility to attack, and the need for verbal means of redress.

Because our face, image, or reputation is so important to us, when we believe it is threatened, we are motivated to take action to alleviate this concern. The way in which these image restoration strategies function to repair one's damaged reputation can be understood through an analysis of the nature of attacks, reproaches, or complaints. Fundamentally, an attack on one's image, face, or reputation is comprised of two components: 1) An act occurred which is undesirable, 2) You are responsible for that action. Only if both of these conditions are believed to be true by the relevant audience is the actor's reputation at risk (and only if the actor perceives that the salient audience believes these two conditions are true is the actor likely to employ image restoration discourse). Let us consider each of these conditions separately.

First, for one's reputation to be threatened, a reprehensible act must have been committed. If nothing bad happened—or if the actor believes that what happened is not considered to be offensive by the salient audience—then the actor's face is not threatened. Furthermore, before actors will be concerned about negative effects on their reputation, they must believe that a salient audience disapproves of the action (it is the actor's perceptions of the audience's beliefs, not their actual beliefs, that prompts defensive discourse). Of course, "action" must be construed broadly, to include words as well as deeds and to include failure to perform expected actions as well as performance of dispreferred actions (in other words, acts of omission as well as commission). It seems reasonable to assume that the more serious the offense—the more vile the action, the more people harmed by it, the longer or more widespread the negative effects, and so forth—the greater the damage to the actor's reputation.

Second, damage to one's face requires that the actor be held responsible for the occurrence of that reprehensible act by the relevant audience. No matter what happened or how terrible it was, it is not reasonable to form an unfavorable impression of a person who is not thought to be responsible for that act. The key point here, of course, is not whether *in fact* the actor caused the damage, but whether the relevant audience *believes* the actor to be the source of the reprehensible act. If a person is thought to be responsible for an act perceived as undesirable, that person's reputation is likely to suffer. Furthermore, perceptions are important here as with offensiveness of the action. Before people are prompted to restore their image, they must believe the audience holds them responsible (for an act they think the audience believes is offensive).

However, just as the undesirability of the act exists on a continuum, responsibility is often not a simple true or false proposition. If several persons jointly committed the act, we might not necessarily hold them all fully responsible, but we may apportion the blame among them. Some (e.g., leaders, instigators, ones who played a particularly important role in commission of the act) might be held to be more responsible for the reprehensible act than others. Furthermore, we tend to hold people more accountable for the effects they intended and to hold them less blameworthy for unintended or unexpected effects. It seems reasonable to assume that a person's reputation will suffer in proportion to the extent to which they are personally or individually held responsible for the undesirable act (including the extent to which they are believed to have intended the act and its consequences).

Viewing the image restoration event in terms of how attacks function explains how image restoration strategies work. Some of the defenses attempt to *deny* that an undesirable act occurred or that the accused was the one who performed it. If no reprehensible act actually occurred (denying that the act actually occurred), the accused's reputation should not be damaged. If the accused did not commit it (either denying that the accused did the deed, or *shifting the blame* for the deed to another), again the accused's face should not be damaged by that action. It is possible that because of the dynamics of attitude formation and change the accused's image may not, even after an effective denial, be restored fully to its level before the attack. However, a successful denial should substantially restore the image.

Another defensive possibility is to attempt to evade or reduce responsibility for the undesirable act. In such cases, one may not be able to completely deny responsibility but may attempt to reduce perceived responsibility for the act. One may claim to have been *provoked* and thus not solely responsible. A person may offer a defense of *defeasibility*, that the action was due to lack of information or ability, and hence not entirely one's own fault. A third possibility is to declare that the action occurred *accidentally*. Or one may claim that the act was performed with *good intentions*. Each of these strategies seeks to reduce the accused's perceived responsibility for the reprehensible act and hence mitigate the damage to reputation from that act. Successful use of strategies to evade responsibility should improve the image of the accused, but may not restore it completely.

It is also possible to reduce the perceived offensiveness of the act through several strategies. *Bolstering* attempts to improve the accused's reputation in hopes of offsetting or making up for the damage to the image from the undesirable act. *Minimization* reduces the magnitude of the negative feelings attributed to the act, in hopes of lessening the ill feelings directed to the accused. *Differentiation* and *transcendence*, in their different ways, attempt to reduce the negative affect associated with the act. *Attacking the accuser*, if the accuser is the injured party, may reduce the audience's sympathy to the injured party, thus lessening the perceptions of the severity of the harmful act. (Incidentally, this strategy may also reduce the impact of the attack by reducing the credibility of the attacker.) *Compensation* is a strategy designed to reduce the perceived severity of the injury. Hence, these strategies all function to reduce the offensiveness of the event. Because the threat to the accused's image should be a function of the offensiveness of the act, successful use of these strategies should help to restore reputation.

The remaining image restoration strategies may be explicable more through cultural norms than through an analysis of the nature of the attack. Most people realize that human beings make mistakes. If a person commits an offense, the offender may come to regret it. The audience may well forgive a person who manages to assure them that, whatever that actor might have done in the past, he or she will take *corrective action*. This may take the form of remedying the problem or promising not to repeat this error (or both). Finally, an actor who engages in *mortification* (an apparently sincere apology, expression of regret, request for forgiveness) may salvage a damaged reputation. These actions can restore, at least partially, the actor's image.

Thus, the workings of many of the image restoration strategies can be explained through an analysis of the essential nature of reproaches or attacks. An attack must portray an act in an unfavorable light and attribute responsibility for that act to the accused. Defenses may attempt to rehabilitate an image by denying or reducing responsibility for that act or by construing the act less negatively (or offsetting its offensiveness). Other defensive strategies (i.e., mortification) may have a more cultural basis. However, I have tried to explain how each should help to restore the accused's image. At this point we are ready to offer a description of verbal image restoration strategies.

TYPOLOGY OF IMAGE RESTORATION STRATEGIES

This desire to offer a typology that is more complete than those found in the rhetorical literature while avoiding the extreme detail found in some descriptions of accounts leads to the list of strategies in this typology of image restoration. Here, image restoration strategies are organized into five broad categories, three of which have variants or subcategories: denial, evading responsibility, reducing offensiveness, corrective action, and mortification. In this discussion I will mention many of the scholars who have dealt with these strategic options, as reviewed in chapters 2 and 3.

Denial

Any person who is forced to defend himself or herself against the suspicions or attacks of others has several options. The speaker may deny performing the wrongful act as Ware and Linkugel (1973) suggest. Goffman (1971) observes that the accused may deny the act occurred or that the accused committed it. Schonbach (1980) suggests that one may claim the failure event did not occur. Schlenker (1980) lists innocence as an option. Tedeschi and Reiss (1981) discuss denial of agency, and Semin and Manstead (1983) mention mistaken identity as a defensive option. Whether the accused denies that the offensive act actually occurred or denies that he or she performed it, either option, if accepted, should absolve the actor of culpability. One strategy for dealing with attacks, then, is simply to deny the undesirable action.

As mentioned in chapter 1, it is possible to reinforce one's denial. For example, after a tape was used to prove that PLO leader Yasser Arafat made derogatory comments about Jews, he claimed that the recording was fabricated ("Arafat Says," 1992). Here, Arafat denied the charge while explaining the apparently incriminating evidence. William Aramony, accused of financial misconduct at United Way, denied those charges and claimed that he was being kept from records that would support his denial (Barringer, 1992). Thus, in addition to denying the charges, he alleged that the evidence he needed to prove his innocence was being withheld. Thus, denial may be supplemented with explanations of apparently damaging facts or lack of supporting evidence.

A popular defense strategy in criminal trials is the alibi. This is basically a witness who testifies that the accused was elsewhere at the time of the crime—and hence cannot have committed the crime. Of course, the effect of an alibi is to provide evidence that—if accepted—denies that the defendant committed the crime.

However, when a person uses denial, others may wonder, "Well if you didn't do it, who did?" Burke (1970) discusses victimage or shifting the blame, and Schonbach (1980) suggests that a form of refusal is applying guilt to another person. This strategy can be considered a variant of denial, because the accused cannot have committed the repugnant act if someone else actually did it. This strategy may well be more effective than simple denial, for two reasons. First, it provides a target for any ill will the audience may feel, and this ill feeling may be shifted away from the accused. Second, it answers the question that may make the audience hesitate to accept a simple denial: "Who did it?"

Evading Responsibility

Those who are unable to deny performing the act in question may be able to evade or reduce their apparent responsibility for it. Four variants of this strategy can be identified. Scott and Lyman's (1968) version of scapegoating—renamed provocation here—suggested that the actor may claim that the act in question was performed in response to another wrongful act, which understandably provoked the offensive act in question. If the other person agrees that the actor was justifiably provoked, the provocateur may be held responsible instead of the actor. Schonbach (1980) and Semin and Manstead (1983) also discussed provocation as an account.

A second strategy for evading responsibility is defeasibility (Scott & Lyman, 1968), pleading lack of information about or control over important factors in the situation. Lack of control seems closely related to Scott and Lyman's notion of biological drives, which is also included under defeasibility. As suggested earlier, subsequent writers (Schonbach, 1980; Tedeschi & Reiss, 1981; Semin & Manstead, 1983) identify a number of variants of defeasibility. Rather than denying that the act occurred, the actor attempts to suggest that lack of information, volition, or ability means that he or she should not be held fully responsible for the act. This strategy, if effective, should reduce the perceived responsibility of the accused for the failure event.

Third, the actor may make an excuse based on accidents (Scott & Lyman, 1968; Tedeschi & Reiss, 1981; or Semin & Manstead, 1983). We tend to hold others responsible only for factors they can reasonably be expected to control. For example, when people are late to a meeting, we may not hold them completely responsible if unforseeable traffic congestion caused their tardiness. Here again, rather than deny that the offensive act occurred, the accused attempts to provide information that may reduce his or her apparent responsibility for the offensive act.

A fourth possibility is for the actor to suggest that performance of the action in question may be justified on the basis of motives or intentions (discussed by Ware & Linkugel, 1973, as a part of denial). Here the wrongful act is not denied, yet the audience is asked not to hold the actor fully responsible because it was done with good, rather than evil, intentions. People who do bad while trying to do good are usually not blamed as much as those who intend to do bad.

Reducing Offensiveness

A person accused of misbehavior may attempt to reduce the degree of ill feeling experienced by the audience. This approach to image repair has six variants: bolstering, minimization, differentiation, transcendence, attacking one's accuser, and compensation. Each one will be briefly explained here.

Bolstering (Ware & Linkugel, 1973) may be used to mitigate the negative effects of the act on the actor by strengthening the audience's positive affect for the rhetor. Here those accused of wrong-doing might relate positive attributes they possess or positive actions they have performed in the past. While the amount of guilt or negative affect from the accusation remains the same, increasing positive feeling toward the actor may help offset the negative feelings toward the act, yielding a relative improvement in the actor's reputation. This strategy might be more effective if the positive traits or actions appear relevant to the accusations or suspicions.

Second, it is possible for the accused to attempt to minimize the amount of negative affect associated with the offensive act. If the rhetor can convince the audience that the negative act isn't as bad as it might first appear, the amount of ill feeling associated with that act is reduced. To the extent this strategy is successful, the person's reputation is restored. Sykes and Matza (1957), Scott and Lyman (1968), Schonbach (1980), Schlenker (1980), Tedeschi and Reiss (1981), and Semin and Manstead (1983) all discuss denial or minimization of injury and/or victim as accounting strategies.

A third possible strategy for minimizing the offensiveness of an action is to engage in differentiation (Ware & Linkugel, 1973). Here the rhetor attempts to distinguish the act performed from other similar but less desirable actions. In comparison, the act may appear less offensive. This may have the effect of lessening the audience's negative feelings toward the act and the actor.

Next, the actor can employ transcendence (Ware & Linkugel, 1973). This strategy for image restoration functions by placing the act in a different context. Ware and Linkugel specifically discuss placing the action in a broader context, but it can also be useful to simply suggest a different frame of reference. For example, Robin Hood might suggest that his actions be viewed not as theft but as assistance to the poor and downtrodden. Similarly, a person accused of wrong-doing might direct our attention to other, allegedly higher values, to justify the behavior in question (Sykes & Matza, 1957; Scott & Lyman, 1968; Schonbach, 1980; Schlenker, 1980; Tedeschi & Reiss, 1981; and Semin & Manstead, 1983, all discuss appeal to values or higher loyalties—or both—as justificative strategies). For example, a police officer could attempt to justify illegally planting evidence on a defendant as the only way to protect society from a dangerous but clever criminal. This positive context may lessen the perceived offensiveness of the act and help improve the actor's reputation.

At times those accused of wrong-doing attack their accusers, as suggested by Rosenfield (1968), Sykes and Matza (1957), Scott and Lyman (1968), Schonbach (1980), and Tedeschi and Reiss (1981) suggested. If the credibility of the source of accusations can be reduced, the damage to one's image from those accusations may be diminished. If the accuser is also the victim of the offensive act (rather than a third party), the apoligist may create the impression that the victim deserved what befell him or her; attacking the accuser may tend to lessen the perceived unpleasantness of the action in question (Semin & Manstead, 1983), again improving the rhetor's reputation. It is also possible that attacking one's accuser may divert the audience's attention away from the original accusation, reducing damage to the rhetor's image.

Compensation is a final potential strategy for reducing the offensiveness of an action (Schonbach, 1980). Here the person offers to remunerate the victim to help offset the negative feeling arising from the wrongful act. This redress may take the form of valued goods or services as well as monetary reimbursement. In effect, compensation functions as a bribe. If the accuser accepts the proffered inducement, and if it has sufficient value, the negative affect from the undesirable act may be outweighed, restoring reputation.

None of these six strategies of decreasing offensiveness denies that the actor committed the objectionable act or attempts to diminish the actor's responsibility for that act. All attempt to reduce the unfavorable feelings toward the actor by increasing the audience's esteem for the actor or by decreasing their negative feelings about the act.

Corrective Action

In this strategy for image restoration, the accused vows to correct the problem. This may take two forms: restoring the situation to the state of affairs before the objectionable action and/or promising to "mend one's ways" and make changes to prevent the recurrence of the undesirable act. If the problem is one that could recur, the actor's position may be enhanced by provision of assurances that changes will prevent it from happening again. Goffman (1971) mentions this possibility as a component of an apology. However, one can take corrective action without admitting guilt, as Tylenol appropriately did in introducing tamper-resistant bottles after their customers were poisoned (Benoit & Lindsey, 1987). The difference between this strategy and compensation is that corrective action addresses the actual source of injury (offering to rectify past damage and/or prevent its recurrence), while compensation consists of a gift designed to counterbalance, rather than to correct, the injury.

Mortification

As Burke (1970, 1973) recognizes, the accused may admit responsibility for the wrongful act and ask for forgiveness, engaging in mortification. If we believe the apology is sincere, we may choose to pardon the wrongful act. Schonbach (1980; see also Goffman, 1971, on apology) also discusses concessions, in which one may admit guilt and express regret. It may be wise to couple this strategy with plans to correct (or prevent recurrence of) the problem, but these strategies can occur independently.

Thus, the rhetor who desires to restore an image through discourse has five basic options: denial, evasion of responsibility, reducing offensiveness, correction, and mortification.* Several of these basic strategies have variants. These strategies for restoring

---

* One possibility I decided to omit, but wanted to mention at least in passing, is the strategic use of silence or ignoring accusations (McLaughlin, Cody, & O'Hair, 1983). The utterance, "I won't dignify that accusation with a reply," is fairly common. There is no question that this approach is used and can be successful. However, I wanted to focus on things a rhetor could *say* or more proactive strategies. This seems to be founded on the hope that if left alone, the image problem may be forgotten. In developing this theory I was interested in describing what verbal steps could be taken to change the audience's perceptions.

sullied reputations are summarized in table 4.1. Having articulated the assumptions supporting this theory and described the strategic options available for image restoration, this chapter most considers three other questions: how the strategies work, the relationship of persuasive attack and defense, and the relationship of this theory to previous work.

A "strategy," as used here, is an abstract or general concept that represents a goal or an effect sought by discourse. An utterance operationalizes a given strategy (see, e.g., Bowers, Ochs, & Jensen, 1993) and can be said to be a specific instance of that strategy. Strategies are thus abstract representations of the relationship between discourse and goals or effects. As discussed earlier, rhetors have goals and they believe (or at least hope) that appropriate discourse can help achieve those goals. Strategy thus represents the discursive intersection between goals sought by a rhetor and effects that may occur in an audience.

These effects may be consummatory or instrumental or both (cf. Festinger, 1957; Fotheringham, 1966), depending upon whether the end sought is an end in itself or a means to another desired end. Utterances may immediately achieve a goal sought by the rhetor (consummatory) or utterances may create effects that are means to achieve a further goal (instrumental). For example, bolstering is probably most often a consummatory strategy: the point of discourse designed to bolster is to influence the audience to have a more favorable impression of the source. Once this source's impression has been bolstered, the discourse has succeeded in accomplishing its goals. Shifting the blame, on the other hand, is better viewed as an instrumental strategy. The immediate effect of (successfully) shifting the blame is to damage the reputation of the other person. However, the ultimate end or goal sought by shifting the blame is to exonerate the source. Thus, this strategy may be viewed as a two-step process: first, the target is blamed for the reprehensible act (the blame is shifted); then, it is hoped, the audience will exonerate the source, restoring the source's reputation. This strategy achieves an immediate effect when the other person is held accountable for the despicable act; it may or may not then achieve its ultimate (instrumental) effect. If the audience agrees that the target should be blamed but continues to hold the source responsible as well, this strategy would probably be judged a failure, because it failed to exonerate the source (even if it succeeded in blaming the target). When it works as intended, however, shifting the blame first achieves a preliminary effect (the target is held responsible for the undesirable act), and then it accomplishes the ultimate effect (the source is cleared of blame).

It is possible that a given utterance has both consummatory and instrumental qualities, serving more than one strategy. For example, there are myriad ways to bolster one's reputation. If a company accused of harming the environment bolsters by discussing its programs of assisting the poor or supporting the fine arts, such discourse may function to bolster its image and would be consummatory. However, if that company chooses instead to enhance its image by touting its environmental programs, this discourse may not only bolster the company's image (consummatory) but also reinforce the company's denial that it had caused environmental problems. This latter strategy can be considered instrumental because bolstering only indirectly denies the charges.

Similarly, one may attempt to defuse charges by attacking one's accuser. Attacking one's accuser may be viewed as an instrumental strategy, because if the credibility of one's accuser can be reduced (the immediate effect of attacking one's accuser), the damage to one's image should be mitigated as well (an instrumental effect). However, in some circumstances it may be possible to shift the blame for the reprehensible act to one's accuser. Such an utterance, then, would function both to attack one's accuser and to shift the blame. In this instance, both strategies are instrumental.

Strategies can, of course, be operationalized in discourse in a multitude of ways, which can make it difficult to identify them. Speakers may not, for example, explicitly note that "I'm trying to shift the blame here." I would argue that the common knowledge and experience critics, rhetors, and audiences share makes identification of utterances possible. There are clues that an analyst may use to try to identify an utterance as an instance of a strategy. The critic may work from the rhetor's perspective, considering the rhetorical problem facing the rhetor and speculating about how an utterance might have been intended by the rhetor to resolve that problem (achieve goals desired by the rhetor). The critic may take the audience's perspective and speculate about how the auditors might react to (or be affected by) a given utterance in that situation. Furthermore, at times the rhetor might give clues in the discourse that help classify an utterance (e.g., the first part of the utterance—"Let me tell you why this problem isn't so bad: it only happens in an unusual set of circumstances that rarely occur"— might be taken as a indication that the speaker is trying to minimize the problem). It may not be possible to identify a given utterance with absolute certainty, but using one or more of these clues (rhetor's goals; audience reactions; discursive evidence) allows critics to make reasonable arguments about the classification of utterances as instances of these strategies.

IMAGE RESTORATION AND THE AUDIENCE

It is important to note that we are dealing with perceptions here. The actor responds to perceived threats to his or her character. These attacks are important to the actor when they are believed to reduce the rhetor's reputation in the eyes of a group (audience) who is salient to the rhetor. As Tedeschi and Reiss put it, "Central to the realization that one faces a predicament is the belief that others attribute to oneself causality and responsibility for the event in question" (1981, p. 271). Of course, the *rhetor's perceptions* of the audience's image of the rhetor may or may not correspond directly to the *audience's actual perceptions* of the rhetor's image. However, the rhetor's perceptions of the audience's reaction to attacks are all the rhetor has available to prompt and guide image restoration efforts. Hence, when trying to understand the rhetor's perception of and response to an attack, critics must consider the rhetor's point of view, the rhetor's perceptions of the audience's beliefs. Of course, if the critic elects to assess the success or effectiveness of the defensive discourse in restoring the rhetor's reputation with the audience, the critic must also consider the audience's actual perception of the rhetor, before and after the image restoration attempt, if possible.

This analysis leads to the idea that in a sense, there are at least two "audiences" for a given image restoration attempt. The apologist addresses an *external audience* consisting of those for whom the accused is most concerned with restoring his or her face. There are three possibilities for this external audience. First, it may consist solely of the person who objected to the apologist's behavior. For example, if Mary criticizes her husband Joe, Joe may wish to restore Mary's impression of him (and be concerned only with Mary's perceptions of him). Here, the rhetor is trying to restore reputation with the accuser. Second, Pat may criticize Chris in front of several coworkers, and Chris may wish to repair Pat's perceptions as well as the perceptions of the other coworkers aware of Pat's charges. In this case, the rhetor is trying to restore reputation with the accuser and others aware of the accusation. A final form of external audience occurs when a third party levels the charges before a relevant group. For example, if an activist protests against a company, that company's spokesperson may wish to reassure customers (and/or stockholders) but be completely (or largely) unconcerned about whether the protester is convinced by the image restoration effort. In this third case, the rhetor is more concerned with restoring reputation with those aware of the accusations than with the accuser. The discussion of effectiveness of speeches in restoring the rhetor's image in chapter 2 seems primarily concerned with the third possibility, trying to get an audience to reject charges of a third party. The discussion of honoring (or accepting) accounts in chapter 3 seems to deal chiefly with the first possibility, mollifying the accuser. Thus, it is important to realize that an apologist's accuser may or may not be part of the audience for whom the image restoration attempt is designed. Similarly, because the accuser may or may not be the alleged victim of the offensive act, rhetors may be concerned primarily with restoring their reputations with victims, or with other audiences, or both.

However, a failure event presumably makes the rhetor feel badly (perhaps embarrassed). Thus, in a certain sense we can consider the rhetor himself or herself to be a second (*internal*) audience, and the accounts and excuses he or she verbalizes may or may not succeed in making the rhetor feel better about her or himself. Snyder and Higgins (1988) review the literature on the effects of excuses on the apologist, reporting that "Given the central role that self-esteem maintenance has been theorized to play in the excuse-making process, it is surprising that only one reported study has directly addressed this issue" (p. 24). McFarland and Ross (1982) suggest that excuse-making may help self-esteem, and Snyder and Higgins report evidence from other studies that "excuses have beneficial affective, performance, and health consequences" (p. 29). Thus, an image defense may have effects on the accuser (who may or may not be the victim of the offensive act), a separate audience (if there is a separate audience, such as customers or stockholders), and on the rhetor uttering the defense.

THE RELATIONSHIP OF ATTACK AND DEFENSE

Ryan (1982) emphasized the importance of understanding image restoration events in the context of the specific attacks provoking the face repair work. This is not to say that before his article, the attacks were completely ignored. However, he was the first to explicitly proclaim the importance of the notion of a speech set. How does the theory of image restoration discourse treat attacks?

Ryan is, of course, correct when he asserts that "the critic cannot have a complete understanding of accusation or apology without treating them both" (1982, p. 254). While he states that there are two types of accusations (against policy and character) and three *stases* of fact—definition, quality, and jurisdiction—(and relates them to Ware and Linkugel's four strategies), he does not discuss the *relationship* between accusation and defense. For example, the apologist may or may not respond to (some or all of) the attacks. It may appear obvious that the rhetor who ignores specifics of the attack cannot hope to be successful, but closer analysis suggests this is not always the case.

First, it is possible to redefine the attack (e.g., to shift from character to policy or from an attack on one issue to an attack on another). For example, Huxman and Linkugel (1988) argue that Huey Long attempted to shift policy accusations from General Hugh Johnson's *kategoria* into character accusations, which were easier for him to handle. Ted Kennedy revealed that he had pled guilty to a charge of leaving the scene of an accident, which helped him transform defense of actions into a defense of character (Benoit, 1988). If the rhetor successfully transforms the accusations, he or she will not respond to them as they were originally developed. This can, at times, be an effective option.

Instead of altering the nature of the accusations, the apologist may attempt to refocus attention on other issues entirely (as Reagan attempted to shift attention away from the arms deal [Heisey, 1988] explains; or as Nixon tried to shift focus away from Watergate [Benoit, 1982]). Although this maneuver does not always work, or may work only for a time, it is a possibility. If successful in reorienting the audience's attention, the rhetor may well be able to successfully ignore some or all of the accusations.

Furthermore, it is possible that all aspects of the accusations may not be equally important to the audience. Thus, it may be to the accused's advantage not to automatically respond to all attacks but to concentrate on those most salient to the audience. It could be a waste of time or even irritating to dwell on attacks that are unimportant to the audience. Additionally, the audience may have forgotten some of the accusations by the time of the response. For example, in the Bitberg controversy, Friedenberg argues that one factor that helped "minimize the accusations of his opponents" was Reagan's "use of time to downplay the entire controversy" (1988, p. 276). Of course, if the charges are particularly salient to the audience, or if they are repeated often enough by the attackers, a rhetor may well be forced to deal with accusations in order to restore his or her reputation. While Ryan (1982) is correct that the critic must consider the accusations, readers must not jump to the conclusion that this means the rhetor must necessarily respond to (all of) the accusations.

It is also possible that there is no clear accusation. The accusation can arise generally in the media, for example, rather than from a rhetor's explicit *kategoria* (see, e.g., Benoit [1988] on Kennedy's Chappaquiddick speech; Brock [1988] on President Ford's pardon; or Ryan [1988b] on Nixon's "Checkers" speech). In such cases, the "attack" may still be important, but more difficult for the critic or analyst to identify.

It is worth noting that several analyses have suggested that attack and defense can become intertwined (see, e.g., Dionisopoulos & Vibbert, 1988; or Lessl, 1988). This seems particularly likely in a series of exchanges, such as in a political campaign. When this happens, it may be inappropriate to label one discourse "the *kategoria*" or attack and the other "the *apologia*" or defense. Indeed, one of the image restoration strategies suggested here is attacking one's accuser(s). Whenever this situation occurs, there would be elements of attack and defense in at least one of the key discourses and quite possibly in all of them. In such cases, the analyst should examine the accusations and responses as they occur in the discourse, rather than trying to characterize a given discourse as *either* an attack *or* a defense.

It should be noted that the strategies outlined here may work just as well with preemptive *apologia*, in which the rhetor attempts to defuse anticipated criticism. Here, the defense would occur before the attack, complicating the relationship between *kategoria* and *apologia*. Indeed, if a preemptive defense were completely successful, no attack would occur. In this instance, the rhetor is "responding" to anticipated accusations rather than actual ones. Thus, while this theory of image restoration discourse acknowledges the importance of considering the accusations, as Ryan (1982) recommends, the relationship between attack and defense is a complex one.

Understanding the basic nature of a persuasive attack helps to explain how (many) defensive strategies function, as suggested earlier. A persuasive attack consists of two basic elements: an offensive act is indicated, and the target of the attack must be held responsible for that act. If the act is not perceived as offensive, no damage to the target's reputation should occur. If the accused is not responsible for the act, again, no damage to the target's image should occur. Hence, image restoration strategies restore images by denying that the rhetor performed the act (or by reducing perceived responsibility for the act) and by reducing the apparent offensiveness of the act. Thus, an understanding of the nature of persuasive attack helps us comprehend persuasive defense, and understanding the nature of specific persuasive attacks helps understand specific defensive responses.

THE THEORY OF IMAGE RESTORATION DISCOURSE AND PREVIOUS RESEARCH

This section discusses the relationship of this theory with other work in the literature. First, it considers each of the major approaches outlined in chapter 2 (Rosenfield [1968], Ware & Linkugel [1973], Burke [1970, 1973], and Ryan [1982]). Next, it discusses the theory's relationship to rhetorical criticism. Then it considers the approach to accounts discussed in chapter 3 (Sykes & Matza [1957], Scott & Lyman [1968], Goffman [1971], Schonbach [1980], Schlenker [1980], Tedeschi & Reiss [1981], and Semin & Manstead [1983]).

It should be obvious that the theory of image restoration discourse is heavily indebted to previous work. I have taken categories directly from the works of the scholars reviewed in chapters 2 and 3. Each made extremely important contributions, which should not be minimized. This means the theory of image restoration discourse is compatible in many regards with much existing research.

Rosenfield's Theory of Mass Media Apology

The theory of image restoration approach is more complete than Rosenfield's (1968) theory. He offers only four characteristics, one of which describes the situation (a "short, intense, decisive clash of views," p. 449), and two of which concern content only generally (facts cluster in the middle; reusing arguments). Invective, or attacking one's opponent, is an option for those attempting to restore their reputations. His theory offers an important starting point, as one would expect in exploratory research. As one might expect in exploratory research, it is incomplete.

Burke's Theory of Guilt

Burke discusses only two strategies for reducing guilt, victimage and mortification (although Brummett [1981], drawing on Burke, adds transcendence). While it is clear that these are important strategic options, they simply do not exhaust the possibilities available for image restoration. Burke discusses the purgative-guilt cycle, in which humans inevitably violate the social order, requiring redemption. Guilt is an important motivation for image restoration.

Burke (1970) sees an important similarity in the way in which mortification and victimage deal with guilt, symbolically "killing" it. Burke suggests that they are both a form of death: mortification a kind of suicide and victimage a kind of homicide (1970, p. 248). I separate these image restoration strategies, however, because of the effects they engender: mortification accepts the blame (placing it on one's "bad" self) and begs forgiveness, while victimage shifts the blame elsewhere, to a scapegoat. Hence, I consider victimage, or shifting the blame, as closer in effect to denial than mortification.

Ware and Linkugel's Theory of Apologia

Ware and Linkugel's (1973) approach offers more strtategies than Rosenfield's or Burke's theories. The four strategies Ware and Linkugel discuss—denial, bolstering, differentiation, and transcendence—are all useful image restoration strategies. Furthermore, they argue that image repair strategies rarely occur singly. The extensive rhetorical criticism stimulated by this approach attests to its utility.

However, it is still incomplete. For example, the strategies of attacking one's opponent, shifting the blame, mortification, minimization, and compensation are not discussed. Furthermore, other writers in this tradition have tried to find other strategies in Ware and Linkugel's (1973) typology. For example, Nelson's (1984) analysis of Billie Jean King's defense argues that "A third bolstering mechanism lay in Billie Jean's efforts to shift the blame" (p. 94). Ware and Linkugel define bolstering as "the obverse of denial" and "any rhetorical strategy which reinforces the existence of a fact, sentiment, object, or relationship . . . viewed favorably by the audience" (1973, p. 277). Hence, shifting the blame (which attempts to persuade the audience that another person actually caused the negative incident) does not seem to be a proper instance of bolstering. Shifting the blame, or victimage, is clearly an important strategy of image restoration but is not part of Ware and Linkugel's typology.

Similarly, Kruse's (1981a) analysis of *apologia* in team sport concludes that "The apologetic responses of sport figures do not differ strategically from the character defenses offered by those in the sociopolitical world" (p. 280). Yet one of her conclusions clearly concerns mortification, which cannot be found in Ware and Linkugel's system: "sport figures are likely to say, 'I'm sorry,' and express regret for their conduct" (p. 281). Nor is this an occasional or minor aspect of sport *apologia*, because she explains that "These apologists verbalize their remorse so frequently that this can be identified as a convention of the discourse" (p. 281). I would agree that the image restoration strategies available to sports figures are no different from the options available to others, and I agree that mortification (expression of remorse and regret) is an important strategy for restoring a tarnished image, but Ware and Linkugel's typology of those possibilities simply does not include mortification.*

A difference between Ware and Linkugel's (1973) theory and the synthesis developed here lies in the treatment of good intentions. They consider good intentions to be simply a part of denial (p. 276). However, I argue that an apologist who says "I did not do the bad thing you accuse me of" is employing a distinctly different approach than one who says "Yes, I did the bad thing you accuse me of, but I didn't intend for any harm to come from it." Aside from the simple fact that only the first utterance actually denies performance of the undesirable action, choosing one over the other clearly limits other utterances. For example, the rhetor who denies

---

* These omissions may well result from the manner in which Ware and Linkugel's strategies were developed. Their four strategies were taken from Abelson's (1959) essay. However, Abelson was not concerned with image restoration, or apologizing, but with "resolution of belief dilemmas," or "intrapersonal conflict resolution" (p. 343). There is no question that these strategies have proven useful in explicating apologetic discourse; the argument here is it should come as no surprise if this typology should not turn out to be exhaustive as to possible image restoration strategies.

committing the act would not benefit from minimizing the harm (after all, he or she didn't do it!). However, minimization works well with good intentions (or denial of bad intent): "I didn't intend any harm, and in fact relatively little harm came from it." Similarly, there is no reason for a person who denies guilt to offer compensation, but one who claims good intentions may reasonably offer to compensate the injured party. Hence, it seems preferable to separate good intentions (or denial of bad intent) from denial.

Another difference between the theory of image restoration and Ware and Linkugel's theory of *apologia* concerns their use of postures. Although they admit that more than one strategy may be present (and much rhetorical criticism since then confirms this), they assert that two will predominate. Perhaps this was true in the speeches they examined to illustrate the initial presentation of their theory, but no conceptual justification was presented for this assertion. In their analysis of Nixon's Watergate rhetoric, they argue that "Within the same speech, he assumed two separate postures" (Harrell, Ware, & Linkugel, 1975, p. 257). How this can be reconciled with their earlier claim that two strategies (one posture) will predominate is never explained. Furthermore, Kahl (1984) argues that in Dean's book *Lost Honor*, differentiation and transcendence predominate, while Ware and Linkugel (1973) declare that one or the other of these—but not both—should predominate in a speech (no posture relies on the combination of differentiation and transcendence; the postures consist of *either* denial *or* bolstering and *either* differentiation *or* transcendence).

While I agree that image repair strategies are often used in combination, I have always found the four stances or postures advanced by Ware and Linkugel (absolutive, vindicative, explanative, and justificative) puzzling. For example, it is not clear how the rhetor who denies that he or she is associated with an action (or object) that repels the audience would benefit from associating that action with a broader, more positive context (transcendence) or from distinguishing it from other similar but less desirable objects (differentiation). If he or she *didn't do it*, what is the point of differentiating or transcending the action? Yet the vindicative posture, one of the four fundamental apologetic postures, employs denial and transcendence, and the absolutive stance combines denial and differentiation. On the other hand, it seems reasonable to me that an apologist might wish to bolster his or her reputation after denying wrong-doing just to make sure. However, there is no stance that relies primarily on denial and bolstering. Therefore, the theory of image restoration, while adopting Ware and Linkugel's four strategies (denial, bolstering, differentiation, and transcendence) as important means for image restoration, eschews their four postures.

A final difference between this theory of image restoration discourse and *apologia* (especially as developed by Kruse, 1981b) concerns its scope. I see no reason to limit image restoration to attacks on character, but argue that defenses against attacks on policy ought to be included with character defenses. One reason policy statements are extremely important is that the stances taken by rhetors help define their public images. Folk wisdom has it that "actions speak louder than words," that policy decisions have more impact on a politician's image than do statements. Stands on controversial issues can without a doubt hurt one's image, as Gold explains: "The candidate's attempt to defend his policy soon becomes an effort to defend his actions and his character, justify his motives and intent—in short, an apologia" (1978, p. 307; see also Ryan, 1982). A person's character is revealed by that person's behavior (policy) and by the behavior (policies) he or she condones or recommends. Hence, it is not easy to disentangle character from policy or to neatly separate defenses of character from defenses of policy.

It is possible that there are some differences between defenses of character and defenses of policy (for example, some strategies might be more effective, in general, for policy than for character). However, I see no reason to believe that the basic *repertoire* of strategies (deny, evade responsibility, bolster, reduce offensiveness, etc.) available to the rhetor who defends character would be different from defenses of policy (especially given their interwoven nature, as just discussed). Similarly, while in most cases I suspect the speech of self-defense will respond to a prior attack, I see no reason why the strategies outlined here could not be used preemptively, to reduce the effectiveness of anticipated attacks.

Ryan's Speech Set Analysis

Ryan's (1982) approach, as suggested in chapter 2, extends Ware and Linkugel in two ways. First, as already discussed, it emphasizes the importance of the attack. This should not be taken as claim that previous writers had completely ignored the attack; however, he was the first one to stress this key point. The theory of image restoration acknowledges the importance of the relationship between attack and defense as well. Second, as just mentioned, both theories include defenses related to policy as well as character. However, the list of potential image restoration strategies proposed here goes beyond Ryan's work.

Other Rhetorical Criticism

What is the relationship of this theory of image restoration discourse to the dozens of instances of rhetorical criticism in the literature? It would be possible to examine each study and recast it into the language of this theory. For example, in Baskerville's (1952) study of Nixon's "Checkers" speech, Nixon's use of a letter from a soldier's wife is discussed. This seems to be a clear example of bolstering. Denial, of course, is the way Nixon handled charges of wrong-doing with the fund. In Jackson's (1956) analysis of Clarence Darrow's discourse, using "invective against the prosecution" and depicting the prosecution as a "tool of some evil force" are clearly instances of attacking the accuser (p. 192, italics omitted). However, while this would make an argument for the exhaustiveness of this system (and I did read the literature with an eye to discovering strategies not included in this system), such an undertaking would not be fair to previous work.

Rhetorical criticism in the last twenty-five years (after the grip of neo-Aristotelian criticism was broken, by forces represented by Black's [1965] book) has been wonderfully diverse. However, other critics' purposes are not always the same as mine, and thus my attempt to reduce their work to my categories would not be appropriate. For example, one of the questions discussed by Haapanen (1988) concerns why President Eisenhower chose to admit that he had approved the U2 overflights after the previous press releases had denied authorization was given. While Eisenhower's motives are an interesting and important question, it lies beyond the scope of this theory of image restoration discourse. Similarly, Farrell and Goodnight's (1981) analysis of discourse arising from the Three Mile Island incident is more concerned with discussing technical versus social communication in public argumentation than with image restoration. Short (1987) applied Ware and Linkugel's theory to Congressman George Hansen's rhetoric. However, he was also interested in discussing Hofstadter's (1965) concept of the "paranoid style" in politics. McGuckin's (1968) analysis of Nixon's "Checkers" speech is arguably as much about rhetorical use of values as about image restoration. To give a final example,

Brummett's (1975) analysis of President Nixon's August 1973 Watergate speech seems to be more concerned with elucidating Burke's concept of substance than his process of purification. Thus, while I have drawn on the body of rhetorical criticism discussed in chapter 2, and while I believe the theory of image restoration discourse developed here can successfully describe part of that work, I do not claim that the theory of image restoration can supplant that work.

Accounts and the Theory of Image Restoration

Some theories of accounts choose not to include apologies or mortification (e.g., Sykes & Matza, 1957; Scott & Lyman, 1968; Schlenker, 1980; Tedeschi & Reiss, 1981; Semin & Manstead, 1983), preferring to focus on excuses and justifications. Thus, the theory of image restoration offers a more complete list of strategies available to the rhetor. However, Goffman (1971) does discuss apologies, and Schonbach (1980) includes concessions in their theories. Only Goffman includes corrective action (and then as a component of apology), despite the fact that plans for correcting the problem can be a very important rhetorical strategy for image restoration that has been unjustly overlooked in the literature (see, e.g., Benoit & Brinson, 1994; Benoit, Gullifor, & Panici, 1991; Benoit & Lindsey, 1987). Thus, although many of the discussions of accounts considered in chapter 3 are more detailed than the theory of image restoration, it includes more general options. Although a matter of preference, I choose to focus at higher levels of abstraction rather than on details of subcategories.

As chapter 3 reveals, many of those who write about accounts have developed much more extensive lists of image restoration strategies than have rhetorical theorists and critics. While this work may include illustrations, unlike rhetorical criticism, their focus tends not to be on the discussion of particular rhetorical artifacts. These writers often incorporate previous lists in their new work, adding further refinements in the form of additional categories and subcategories. For example, Scott and Lyman (1968) discussed defeasibility, which concerns lack of knowledge or will, as a possible accounting strategy. Tedeschi and Reiss (1981, p. 282) break this category down into failure to foresee consequences (with eight subcategories, including both "mistake" and "inadvertancy") and lack of volition (including four physical and six psychological varieties).

A limitation of these lists is that their complexity renders them unwieldy. It would be fruitless to deny, for example, that a rhetor can develop defeasibility as an account in a variety of ways (just as a rhetor can bolster in many different ways), but it seems preferable to me to simply group these variants of defeasibility together, rather than list drugs, alcohol, illness, and so forth as separate subcategories. Unless we have evidence that, say, drugs is a more readily acceptable excuse than alcohol, how important is it to devote separate categories to these variants of defeasibility? Similarly, Schonbach (1980) distinguishes between accounts based on past restitution or compensation and those based on future restitution or compensation. It is not clear what advantage is gained from this distinction. We could also divide such offers in other ways (e.g., compensation worth less, the same, or more than the injury), but these sorts of choices add possibly needless intricacy. If we had evidence that, for example, future compensation was more (or less) persuasive than past compensation, this could be a useful distinction. However, it is not clear how the lists of image restoration strategies benefit from some of the fine nuances of these lists of accounts.

Of course, those who desire extremely detailed lists of these strategies can consult Schonbach (1990), who lists almost one hundred and fifty categories and subcategories, or other writers described in chapter 3. There is certainly a place for such exhaustive analyses. However, I find it more useful to list image restoration strategies at a higher level of abstraction. Taking this approach results in a list of image restoration strategies that is exhaustive at a more general level and is arguably easier to conceptualize. It is clearly a matter of preference and convenience rather than a theoretical or a conceptual advantage, though.

CONCLUSION

This chapter articulated and discussed a theory of image restoration discourse that pursues the identity objective by drawing on the diverse sets of literature briefly reviewed in chapters 2 and 3. Two key assumptions are outlined (communication is goal-driven, identity maintenance is a key goal of communication), and a list of strategies for restoring reputation is developed. An analysis of reproaches or attacks is put forward to explain how many of the strategies function, and cultural mores are used to explain the remaining strategy (i.e., mortification). The implications of Ryan's *kategoria-apologia* speech set are discussed.

Of course, this theory is relatively limited in its domain. It does not address related questions, such as the initial development of a positive image or reputation. Similarly, while acknowledging the importance of persuasive attack (and discussing its two basic elements), it does not develop a typology of attacking strategies. Furthermore, for those desiring a detailed list of specific strategic options, some of the analyses reviewed in chapter 3 are superior. Nevertheless, the theory of image restoration is developed as an aid to understanding an important form of human communication.

The next four chapters provide illustrative applications of this theory. Chapter 5 concerns advertisements by Coca-Cola and Pepsi-Cola in a trade publication, *Nation's Restaurant News*. It illustrates the interactive give-and-take attack and defense between two parties, and does so in the advertising context. The next two chapters concern corporate image restoration rhetoric designed to control damage after disastrous incidents. Chapter 6 concerns Exxon's image restoration strategies after the Exxon *Valdez* oil spill, and chapter 7 investigates Union Carbide's efforts to restore its reputation after the gas leak in Bhopal, India. Finally, chapter 8 analyzes President Nixon's image restoration efforts after announcing his decision to send troops into Cambodia. This illustrates the relationship between policy and character and shows how a defense of image may occur before an anticipated attack (preemptively).

The procedure adopted in each of these applications was similar. First, texts of the defensive utterances (and, except for chapter 8, attacking discourses) were collected and closely analyzed. Consideration of the backgrounds of these incidents provided insights into which issues or topics would probably become important. The categories listed in table 4.1 were used to identify instances of image restoration strategies in the defensive discourse. Then the strategies employed were evaluated in terms of their appropriateness considering the attack (except for the preemptive discourse examined in chapter 8) and the apparent audience. Where available, empirical evidence of the effects of the discourse was used to confirm (or disconfirm) the evaluation offered.

Table 4.1. Image Restoration Strategies

Denial
    Simple denial
    Shifting the blame

Evading of Responsibility
    Provocation
    Defeasibility
    Accident
    Good intentions

Reducing Offensiveness of Event
    Bolstering
    Minimization
    Differentiation
    Transcendence
    Attack accuser
    Compensation

Corrective Action

Mortification

---

5   The Cola Wars: Coke versus Pepsi

In this chapter I apply the theory of image restoration discourse to a series of advertisements by Coke and Pepsi in the trade publication *Nation's Restaurant News*. First, I describe the background of this controversy. Then I describe three years of advertisements. This is followed by a criticial analysis (applying the strategies of image restoration) and an evaluation of Coke and Pepsi's attack and defense. Evidence of the effectiveness of their advertisements is examined, and implications for image restoration discourse are described. This application is different from the others to follow because it studies an exchange of multiple messages that include both persuasive attack and defense from the two parties.

BACKGROUND OF THE CONTROVERSY

Coca-Cola and Pepsi-Cola have been fierce competitors for many years. Coke fought Pepsi, while Diet Pepsi battled Diet Coke. Pepsi issued the "Pepsi Challenge" and enlisted Michael Jackson in its cause (see, e.g., Enrico & Kornbluth, 1986). Coke counterattacked with "New Coke," and, when it was plain that the demand for their old Coke hadn't been quenched, it struck again with "Classic Coke." Coke mustered another Michael—Michael Jordan—to fight for its product. Recently, this battle for cola supremacy reached new heights of attack and defense, as Coke and Pepsi crossed pens in a series of advertisements in the pages of a trade publication, *Nation's Restaurant News*. Although most consumers didn't see this advertising campaign, which was aimed at those who sell fountain soft drinks, consumers would feel the fallout from the battle whenever they dined out.

Fountain sales are an important market segment, totaling nearly $10 billion per year. This translates to about 30 percent of Coca-Cola's sales and about 20 percent of Pepsi-Cola's revenues (Konrad & DeGeorge, 1991). Furthermore, fountain sales are believed to be important in building brand loyalty. Rick Routheir, general manager of Pepsi's national sales, explains that "whenever a customer wants a Pepsi and can't get one, it's bad for business" (Konrad & DeGeorge, 1991, p. 71). Thus, the soft drink fountain sales market is a significant one, and advertisements in a trade publication aimed at this market deserve critical attention. This essay offers a rhetorical analysis of three years of advertisements by Coke and Pepsi in *Nation's Restaurant News* as they fought for supremacy in the fountain soft drink business. Description and analysis of the advertisements will be followed by an assessment of the advertisement campaigns.

THE ADVERTISEMENTS OF COKE AND PEPSI

Advertisements by Coke and Pepsi in *Nation's Restaurant News* from 1990 to 1992 were selected for analysis. These are summarized in table 5.1. Each advertisement was given a code because some were run more than once (and, in some cases, run again with very minor changes). Although some of the advertisements are independent, some are clearly persuasive responses to attacks from the other company. Therefore, this analysis will describe these persuasive messages chronologically.

The first advertisement from Coke (C1, "We don't cut the cord," January 22, 1990) begins by asserting that "After we install your fountain equipment, we don't cut the cord." It stresses Coke's service commitment to its customers, describing the "Coca-Cola Customer Communications Center" and its twenty-four-hour, seven-days-a-week 800 telephone number. The ad promises that local service can be obtained "within minutes" (p. 24). It also emphasizes that Coca-Cola equipment is tested to prevent maintenance problems from occurring. An advertisement quite similar to this ran in May (C1a, "Deliver more than syrup," May 14, 1990).

The first Pepsi advertisement (P1, "First place," January 22, 1990), entitled "FIRST PLACE. PREFERRED TASTE," provides a direct comparison of Diet Pepsi and Diet Coke. The ad boasts that Diet Pepsi won in a "National Fountain Taste Test" because "it tastes better and has more real cola flavor." The risk to fountain operators is sketched to make certain that the implications of this argument are understood: "don't let your customers go somewhere else to get the taste they want" (p. 23). This ad was run for four consecutive issues (January 22 and 29, February 5 and 12, 1990).

In February, Coca-Cola began its counterattack. First, it ran an ad to respond directly to Pepsi's taste test claims (C2, "3 cold, hard facts," February 26, 1990). This message announced that it contained "3 COLD, HARD, FACTS ABOUT WHO'S NUMBER 1." Readers learn that Coke outsells Pepsi about two to one, Diet Coke beats Diet Pepsi about three to one, and Sprite leads Slice four to one. "These are big numbers that let you know what consumers enjoy most— Coca-Cola brands." Coke spells out the implications for those who make a living from fountain sales: "the cold hard fact is, that giving your customers what they want means bigger profits for you" (p. 22). This message provides a direct response to Pepsi's taste-test claims.

The second part of Coke's response came the next week (C3, "Satisfy customers' hunger," March 21, 1990) in the form of a four-page ad attacking Pepsi. The first page asks, "Is your soft-drink supplier satisfying your customers' hunger instead of their thirst?" and suggests that "Perhaps it's time to question your choice of a soft-drink supplier" (p. 19). This tactic should attract the attention of retailers.

The second page of this advertisement contains statements and statistics to support the claim that Pepsi threatens the business of other restaurants and fast-food establishments. Pepsi has "admitted that a top priority has been the growth of its own restaurant business," and in 1989, Pepsi's restaurant business increased 16.3 percent. Coke presents statistics claiming that 83 percent of the increase in customer visits to Pepsi restaurants came at the expense of other fast-food restaurants. It "owns more quick-service restaurants than anybody else" and "spends nearly $250 million in advertising directed against your business." Specifically, Pizza Hut "is the leading pizza chain with a 20 percent share," "Taco Bell leads the U.S. Mexican restaurant category with a 57 percent share," and "Kentucky Fried Chicken has a 47 percent share" of the fried chicken market. The overall claim is that "If a PepsiCo restaurant is your competition, every time you serve Pepsi, you're pouring money into your competitor's pocket" (p. 20).

The third page stresses Coke's advantages and repeats the sales comparisons from "3 cold, hard facts" (Sprite over Slice four to one; Coke over Pepsi two to one; and Diet Coke over Diet Pepsi three to one). The advertisement stresses that, unlike Pepsi, "Coca-Cola's Number One Business is Soft-Drinks" and that it "does not compete with you in any way" and suggests that readers should "Grow your profits, not your competition's" (p. 21). Profits are, of course, the bottom line for Coke's audience.

The last page asks, "If PepsiCo's restaurant business is growing at your expense, why would you help pay for that expansion by pouring PepsiCo products at your fountain?" The advertisement ends by declaring that Coca-Cola offers "Commitment, not competition" (p. 22). The attack on Pepsi is unmistakable, and Pepsi's threat to those who buy syrup for their fountain soft drinks is made completely clear. This ad was also inserted December 10, 1990.

No more advertisements appeared for two months, when Pepsi struck back with a three-page spread (P2, "'Mc'Coke," May 7, 1990). The first page began with "'Mc'Coke" in large print, followed by the suggestion that readers should "Make no mistake about it: We all know where Coke's commitment really is" (p. 57). The next page refers to Coke's recent ads and declares that "Coke is committed to McDonald's success. And we doubt they'll help *you* succeed at McDonald's expense." This was followed by a series of questions: Coke gives more money to McDonald's than other retailers—don't you think that hurts your business? Do you think Coke would offer promotions first to you or McDonald's? Do you think they'd respond first to your service calls or those of McDonald's? The advertisement declares that McDonald's is Coke's biggest customer, and their commitment is to McDonald's. "To Coke, if you're not McDonald's, your business may mean McNothing" (p. 58). The last page stresses five advantages of Pepsi: technological superiority, service, local suppliers, preferred taste, and marketing. Thus, Pepsi seeks to turn Coke's charges of competition against them. This ad ran the next week as well (May 14, 1990).

Coke ran the copy for "We don't cut the cord" (C1) with two changes on May 14, 1990 (C1a/2, "Deliver more than syrup"). It was prefaced with a page entitled "Shouldn't your soft-drink supplier deliver more than just syrup?" Then the two pages from C1 followed. The "3 cold, hard facts" advertisement (C2) was appended to the end of this four-page advertisement.

Pepsi offered a two-page persuasive message designed to deny Coke's accusations (P3, "Won't change competition," May 21, 1990) the next week. In it, Pepsi asserts that "Choosing a soft drink supplier won't change your competitive environment. But your choice of a soft drink partner *will* affect your ability to compete" (pp. 60–61). It seems clear that this ad is an attempt to defuse Coke's charges that Pepsi competes with its customers.

The cola wars cooled off a bit at this point. Coke ran an advertisement asserting that it provides "Technology that improves your cash flow" (C4, "Improves cash flow," June 4, 1990, p. 31). Another ad stressed Coke's promotions—in this case, the Coca-Cola "MagiCup" (C5, "MagiCup," September 17, 1990; October 8, 1990). The title of this advertisement explains that "Sometimes all it takes to make your business grow is a little magic" (p. 23). Pepsi offers four advantages in its next message: service, technology, marketing, and taste (P4, "Commitment you can count on," October 1, 1990). Pepsi then ran advertisements with quotations from satisfied customers (P5, "A few quotes," October 22, 1990; November 12, 1990). These suggest that "Before you select a soft drink supplier, get a few quotes" (p. 14). Coke expresses its appreciation of its customers (C6, "Thanks to customers," November 26, 1990; December 17, 1990) and suggests that readers should "Invest in the liquid asset that yields the most profit" (C7, "Liquid assets = profits," December 17, 1990, p. 25). Pepsi used the idea of quotations from satisfied customers again, but with different quotes (P5a, "A few [more] quotes," December 17, 1990). In February Pepsi repeated the four advantages from October: service, technology, marketing, taste (P6, "Count on Pepsi," February 11, 1991). However, at this point the cola wars began to heat up again, with each company firing direct salvos at the other.

Pepsi ran a three-page advertisement (P6, "Accounts payable/receivable," March 11, 1991) explicitly attacking Coke. The first page declares that "Judging by the latest figures, Coke classifies its restaurant accounts into two distinct categories" The next page lists "Accounts Receivable" with corporate logos from Jack in the Box, Long John Silvers, Popeye's, Rax, Red Lobster, Olive Garden, Friendly, Hardee's, Sonic, Roy Rogers, Carl's Jr., Burger King, Fuddruckers, Baskin Robbins, and Wendy's (all Coke accounts). The third page lists McDonald's logo under "Accounts Payable." The text asserts that "We figure last year, Coke reaped record profits from accounts like yours—while they lost money on their largest account. And this year, while Coke required national accounts like you to absorb a per-gallon price increase, we hear *there was no change to McDonald's net price.*" If this wasn't clear enough, the message emphasizes that "In effect, Coke's pricing policy is requiring you to subsidize the operations of your largest competitor" (p.

34). No business would want to subsidize its competitors. This ad ran again two weeks later (March 25, 1991).

Coke's response came in the form of an open letter from Charles S. Frenette, senior vice president and general manager (C8, "Open letter," April 28, 1991). Although the text occupies but a single page, the facing page was blank red, dramatically calling attention to this message. This letter charges that "PepsiCo has stepped beyond the bounds of acceptable competitive behavior" and that "many within the food service industry have urged us to reply" to Pepsi's charges. Charges that Coke increased prices for some customers but not others and that Coke lost money on its largest account "were absolutely false." While Coke did institute a price increase, it was applied "to all customers, from the largest to the smallest." It was "universally applied; there were no exceptions." Frenette also denies that Coke lost money on McDonald's: "we continued to enjoy a healthy and profitable relationship with even our largest customers" (p. 24). Thus, Pepsi's claims that Coke charged other accounts more than McDonald's, that it lost money on McDonald's, and that other accounts subsidized McDonald's were all forcefully denied.

The open letter did not stop at denying Pepsi's charges. Frenette reported that "we notified PepsiCo management in the strongest terms that their advertisement was false. After PepsiCo ran a *second advertisement* with the same false claims, we decided we must reply in this public forum" (p. 25, italics original). Thus, not only did Pepsi make false accusations against Coke in the first ad, they ran the charges again *knowing* that they were false. Frenette contrasts this with the claim that "Coca-Cola Fountain has built its business on the trust of over 350,000 retail outlets throughout the United States...by consistently dealing with all of our customers fairly, equitably, and ethically for over 105 years" (p. 25). While he stops short of directly labeling Pepsi's behavior unfair, inequitable, and unethical, the implication is unmistakable.

Finally, Frenette stresses that "Our approach to business reflects The Coca-Cola Company's commitment to maximizing your profitability by bringing you the best brands, unsurpassed service, and superior account management *while not competing for your customers*" (p. 25, italics original). After denying Pepsi's charges, revealing that Pepsi had knowingly published false charges in (at least) the second advertisement, and emphasizing Coca-Cola's trust and ethics, Frenette returns to Coke's fundamental attack on Pepsi: Pepsi's restaurant business directly competed with those who bought Pepsi fountain soft drinks.

Coke's next advertisement returns to the theme that Coke outsells Pepsi (C9, "Heart of the matter," April 29, 1991). The headline is "LET'S GET TO THE HEART OF THE MATTER." The ad then observes that Coke leads Pepsi almost two to one, Diet Coke outsells Diet Pepsi almost four to one, and Sprite leads Slice by fourteen to one. The persuasive message stresses that Coca-Cola brands are the ones "consumers enjoy most" and that "the heart of the matter is that giving your customers what they want means bigger profits for you" (p. 35). This ad makes the argument that Coke products outsell those from Pepsi and that this means greater profits for fountain retailers.

Following the profits theme, in May Coke ran an advertisement declaring that "soft drinks can impact your bottom line" (C10, "Bottom line," May 20, 1991, p. 92). Here the argument is that when customers leave without buying a soft drink, profits are lost. The ad promises that "With Coca-Cola Fountain as your soft drink partner, you get the commitment, knowledge, and resources to help you sell *even more* soft drinks" (p. 93, italics original). This ad was inserted again in slightly modified form several months later (October 7, 1991).

Pepsi's next advertisement poses the question, "Who's really winning the cola wars?" (P7, "Who's winning," May 20, 1991, p. 37). The first answer is that "You [the retailer] are" (p. 38), because the focus is on the customer and service. However, later the claim is modified to assert that "you and Pepsi are winning the cola wars, together" (p. 39). In the midst of the copy is the statement that "we work hard to understand restaurants and become your total business partner" (p. 39), which could be a justification for Pepsi's movement into the food industry, but this argument is not fully developed here.

Coke then returns to the theme of competition, asking its own question: "IS PEPSI FISHING IN YOUR POND?" (C11, "Pepsi's fishing your pond," July 15, 1991, p. 34). Pepsi's diversification into the food service industry is characterized as its "Long-Term Strategy." Coke stresses that "Pepsi has poured $800 million—40 percent of its entire capital spending—into its restaurant business, which consists of over 19,500 Taco Bell, Pizza Hut, and KFC outlets worldwide." The impact on other retailers is explained: "Pepsi is draining your labor pool, driving up real estate costs, and taking away your store traffic." It ends by predicting that Pepsi's "restaurant business, like a good fish story, will keep getting bigger." This ad was also run on August 26, 1991.

In October, Pepsi returned to the question of Coke's relationship with McDonald's (P8, "Driving traffic," October 7, 1991). The copy declared that "When it comes to driving traffic, Coke follows one basic rule...Never cross the yellow lines" (pp. 4748). The second and third pages of this message reproduce the "golden arches" of McDonald's, and the argument is that *"McDonald's is Coke's biggest* and most important account. If Coke brings you marketing programs that drive traffic to your store, that would mean taking customers away from McDonald's. That's something Coke can never do" (p. 48, italics original). The ad also asserted that Pepsi will provide resources to bring customers into restaurants, but Coke will not. This message was inserted again the next month (November 18, 1991).

Another response to Coke's competition attack emerged in November (P9, "Pepsi is committed," November 18, 1991). The advertisement observes that "While Coke is busy telling you Pepsi isn't committed to its customers, Pepsi customers will tell you something else" (p. 40). This is followed by a testimonial from Craig MacDonald of Round Table Pizza. He acknowledged that PepsiCo owns Pizza Hut, but states that "I can't say enough about Pepsi's attention to detail and the overall level of service" (p. 42). This is designed to reassure those who worry about Coke's charges that Pepsi competes with its own customers.

Coke next placed a four-page insert (C12, "Competition/commitment," November 11, 1991) charging that "ONE SOFT DRINK SUP-PLIER IS IN COMPETITION WITH YOUR BUSINESS. ONE IS COMMITTED TO IT" (p. 37). Again Coke marshals impressive facts and figures to support its case: Pizza Hut is the number one pizza chain, with 24 percent of the market, Taco Bell is number one in the Mexican restaurant market with 70 percent; KFC has 50 percent of the quick-service chicken business; and Pepsi just bought a hamburger chain, Hot'n Now. Coke argues that "nearly half of the 1990 business growth in these restaurants came at your expense" and that "every time you sell a Pepsi soft drink, you're funding PepsiCo's restaurant. And pouring money into your competitor's pockets" (p. 38). Coke repeats the figures on Coke and Pepsi (almost two to one), Diet Coke and Diet Pepsi (over two to one), and Sprite and Slice (9 to 1). The advertisement ends by stressing the benefits of Coca-Cola commitment: "Coca-Cola trademark, account management, dispenser repair, dispensing equipment, quality assurance,

flexible distribution, consumer marketing, superior product line"
(p. 40).

Quite a hiatus occurred in 1992. In May, Pepsi declared that "In
an unprecedented event, Pepsi and Coke finally agree" (P10,
"Pepsi & Coke agree," May 11, 1992, p. 33). Here Pepsi develops
the argument that was implicit in its "Who's winning" (P7) ad:
"Coke says Pepsi restaurant experience will have a serious impact
on your business. They're right. Just ask Subway" (pp. 34–35). Fred
DeLuca, president and founder of Subway, reported that "We also
have a terrific partnership with Pepsi. Their restaurant experience
is very valuable" (p. 34). The testimonial also reveals that "Pepsi
wants us to succeed. They help us promote, and they are committed to helping us grow" (p. 35). This ad is different from "A few
quotes" (P5), because this one not only quotes from Pepsi's customers but argues that Pepsi's restaurant experience is an asset.
This advertisement was repeated twice (in two- instead of three-
page spreads) on August 3 and September 21, 1992.

The competition charge appears again in Coke's next offering
(C13, "Beef with PepsiCo," May 11, 1991). The headline declared
that "IF YOU SELL HAMBURGERS, NOW YOU HAVE A BEEF WITH PEPSICO"
(p. 15). This message concerns Pepsi's purchase of the Hot'n Now
hamburger restaurant chain. The copy stresses the threat this
move presents: "In the next year alone, PepsiCo plans on opening
100 new Hot'n Now units. Of course, this could just be the beginning." The impact on retailers is made explicit: "every Pepsi you
pour contributes to the growth of one of PepsiCo's nearly 21,000
restaurants," including Pizza Hut, Taco Bell, and Kentucky Fried
Chicken. In contrast, Coke promises it "works with you, not
against you," because "our only business is to help you sell more
soft drinks." Furthermore, the ad stresses that "when we make
money, we don't go out and buy restaurants to compete with you.
We invest in the technology, service, and innovations that will
make your profits grow." Although other ads had stressed Pepsi's
use of profits from soft drink fountain sales to buy more restaurants, this is the first one to make the contrast here explicit (*we
don't use profits to buy competing restaurants; we invest in serving
you better*).

The next week Coke's three-page spread (C14, "Bag of
money," May 18, 1992) shows a drawing of a case of Coca-Cola
fountain syrup, declaring that "THERE'S ONLY ONE WAY WE CAN MAKE
THIS BOX OF SYRUP INTO A BAG OF MONEY. TOGETHER" (pp. 93–94). The
message stresses Coke's "Integrated Beverage System," which pro-

vides flexible delivery, quality, technology to improve profits, immediate repair service, a product customers prefer, and marketing programs. This advertisement was also placed in inserts in the August 24, 1992, and October 12, 1992, issues.

This theme continues in the next message (C15, "Profits flow," September 21, 1992), which features a picture of a Coca-Cola cup filled with soft drink and ice: "TOGETHER, WE CAN MAKE THE PROFITS FLOW FROM THIS CUP" (p. 15). The "Integrated Beverage System" is touted again, although not in as much detail. It stresses that "By working together, as partners, we both prosper. Your customers enjoy the quality drinks they want, you make a maximum profit, and we create a successful future together." While Pepsi is not mentioned in the ad, this and the "Bag of money" ad emphasize Coke and the retailer working together, which could be seen as a contrast to Pepsi's competition. This ad was also run on November 30, 1992.

The last advertisement in 1992, from Coke, repeats the charge that Pepsi competes with its customers (C16, "Adios Pepsi," December 21, 1992). The copy reveals that "Taco Bell is selling hamburgers. So when are you going to say adios to PepsiCo?" (p. 87). It mentions Hot'n Now again, along with Pepsi's purchase of California Pizza Kitchen and Carts of Colorado. Readers learn that Taco Bell is selling hamburgers in test markets. The advertisement explains that "Obviously, there's a pattern here. Every year, PepsiCo takes a bigger share of your restaurant business. And every dollar you pay for Pepsi syrup contributes to PepsiCo's expansion." Coke, on the other hand, portrays itself as a partner rather than a competitor.

These, then, are the volleys fired in the cola wars in the pages of *Nation's Restaurant News*. Some advertisements bolster the two companies' images, while others directly attack the other company. Some can be best understood as defensive messages, replying to persuasive attacks. The next two sections will analyze the defensive strategies employed in these campaigns and then evaluate the two campaigns.

CRITICAL ANALYSIS OF PERSUASIVE ATTACK
AND DEFENSE IN THE COLA WARS

In a series of messages such as an advertising campaign, individual messages cannot always be simply categorized as *either* attacking *or* defending messages. Often messages will contain both elements. The fact that an important defensive strategy is to attack one's accuser adds additional difficulties to such attempts. While individual messages may resist such classification, nevertheless broad attacking and defensive strategies can be identified; this section will do so.

Persuasive Attacks

Pepsi's "First place" (P1) ad can be considered the first attack in this series of advertisements. Here, the quality of Pepsi's product is claimed to be superior to Coke's. Pepsi attacks Coke more directly with its "'Mc'Coke" (P2), "Accounts payable/receivable" (P6), and "Driving traffic" (P8) messages. These advertisements accuse Coke of favoring McDonald's over other customers. The "Accounts payable/receivable" (P6) messages were by far the most vicious.

Coke's primary accusation is that Pepsi's restaurants compete with its own customers. Coke attacks Pepsi with its "Satisfy customers' hunger" message (C3), arguing that Pepsi is directly competing with those who buy soft drink fountain products from it. This is followed by further attacks in the same vein: "Pepsi's fishing your pond" (C11), "Competition/commitment" (C12), "Beef with PepsiCo" (C13), and "Adios Pepsi" (C16). Its "3 cold, hard facts" message (C2, C1a/2) pales in comparison but is in fact more direct than Pepsi's "First place" advertisement. Coke's strongest attack, of course, comes in its "Open letter" (C8), accusing Pepsi of making false accusations and repeating them after being told they were false.

Persuasive Defense

It might appear that Coke's "3 cold, hard facts" (C2) is a denial. However, it never actually denies that Pepsi won the taste test. It is probably better understood as an instance of transcendence. Rather than compare colas on the basis of reactions to taste tests, Coke implies, consider the more important question of who sells the most cola. On the basis of this quite different criterion, Coke is the real winner. Of course, Coke does issue an extremely forceful denial in its "Open letter" (C8). Coke's messages bolster its image by repeating the sales comparisons and stressing Coke's advantages as a supplier of fountain soft drinks. Coke also attacks its accuser, which can be a defensive strategy.

Pepsi denies Coke's charges in "Won't change competition" (P3), which also bolsters Pepsi's image by stressing its advantages. The testimonials ("A few quotes," P5; "A few [more] quotes," P5a; "Pepsi & Coke agree," P10, P10a) function both to deny Coke's charges and bolster its image. Pepsi also bolsters its image by stressing its advantages as a fountain soft drink supplier. Its ads on commitment to customers ("Commitment you can count on," P4; "Pepsi is committed," P9) also function to bolster its image. Pepsi also attacks its accuser, another defensive strategy.

EVALUATION OF COKE AND PEPSI'S COLA WARS

This evaluation will take up several topics. First, it explains that both advertising campaigns did a good job explaining the relevance of their arguments to their audience. Second, it argues that Coke's campaign was superior to Pepsi's in several ways.

Strengths of the Campaigns

Both companies admirably explain the impact or answer the "So what?" question. For example, in "First place" (P1), Pepsi warns retailers against letting their "customers go somewhere else to get the taste they want" (January 29, 1990, p. 23). Pepsi's "Accounts payable/receivable" advertisement (P6) declares that "Coke's pricing policy is requiring you to subsidize the operations of your largest competitor" (March 11, 1991, p. 34). Coke's "3 cold, hard facts" advertisement (C2) explains that "giving your customers what they want means bigger profits for you" (February 6, 1990, p. 6). The "Satisfy customers' hunger" ad from Coke (C3) asks "Why would you help pay for" Pepsi's restaurant "expansion by pouring PepsiCo products at your fountain?" (March 2, 1990, p. 22). The ad "Pepsi's fishing your pond" (C11) admonishes retailers that "Pepsi is draining your labor pool, driving up real estate costs, and taking away your store traffic" (July 15, 1991, p. 34). Similarly, "Beef with PepsiCo" (C13) argues that "every Pepsi you pour contributes to the growth of one of PepsiCo's nearly 21,000 restaurants" (May 11, 1991, p. 15). The implications of the claims advanced in both sets of advertisements were generally well-developed.

Superiority of Coke's Campaign

Coke's attack and defense were generally better designed than Pepsi's persuasive messages. The most egregious example, of course, is Pepsi's "Accounts payable/receivable" spread (P6), which contained false accusations. As if this weren't enough, these lies were repeated after Pepsi was informed of their falsity.* It seems highly unwise to make such allegations without proof. The fact that Pepsi continued to make false charges against Coke means that it wasn't a mistake but an intentionally malicious attack. Thus, this exchange can only be expected to damage Pepsi's image and credibility. Coke's attacks on Pepsi as competing with its customers (C3, C11, C12, C13, C16) were generally more persuasive than Pepsi's other attacks (P2, P8) because there is no reason to believe Coke's relationship with its largest customer is as strong as Pepsi's ownership of its fast-food restaurants.

Second, Coke's persuasive messages seemed to offer more and better support for their claims. For example, in the "Satisfy customers' hunger" advertisement (C3), Coke does an impressive job of marshaling its facts and arguments against Pepsi. We have statistics on Pepsi's restaurant traffic growth (16.3 percent), and we are even told how much came from other fast-food restaurants (83 percent). Coke reports on the amount of restaurant advertising Pepsi contracts ($250 million). We are given market shares for pizza (Pizza Hut: 20 percent), Mexican food (Taco Bell: 57 percent), and fried chicken (KFC: 47 percent). Competition/commitment (C12) is equally impressive. While shorter, "Pepsi's fishing your pond" (C11), "Beef with PepsiCo" (C13), and "Adios Pepsi" (C16) also contain statistics and/or concrete examples. Pepsi's "'Mc'Coke" advertisement (P2), on the other hand, offers speculation instead of statistics: "we doubt they'll help *you* succeed at McDonald's expense"; do you think Coke would give you or McDonald's new promotions first; do you think Coke would respond first to your service needs or those of McDonald's? Coke offers statistical evidence (83 percent) of the impact of Pepsi's food business on other fast-food restaurants, while Pepsi asserts that Coke gives more to

---

*I can't verify that Pepsi's charges were false. However, surely Pepsi wouldn't have let Coke accuse them of making false charges if Pepsi could have substantiated them. Perhaps more importantly, when Coke labeled the charges as false without comment by Pepsi, the magazine's readers surely would have assumed that the charges were false.

McDonald's and asks if the retailers think this affects their business. "Driving traffic" offers mere assertions: "If Coke brings you marketing programs that drive traffic to your store, that would mean taking customers away from McDonald's. That's something Coke can never do" (October 7, 1991, p. 48). Why not?

Apart from the clear-cut difference in supporting material (fact versus innuendo), Pepsi's arguments are surprisingly weak. If retailers buy Pepsi's premise that financial interest drives customer support and think that Coke *might* send service to McDonald's first, they must be *certain* that Pepsi would send service to Pizza Hut, Taco Bell, or KFC first. Pepsi's financial interest in the restaurants it *owns* is far greater than Coke's interest in McDonald's. Similarly, Pepsi's "Driving traffic" message (P8) simply asserts that Coke would never drive traffic from McDonald's to other fast-food outlets. No explanation or support for this claim is provided. Why would it matter to Coke whether a customer bought a Coke in McDonald's or in Burger King? A purchase of Coke should generate the same profit to Coke regardless of where it occurs. However, it should matter a great deal to Pepsi whether a Pepsi is bought in a Pizza Hut (which it owns, so Pepsi would profit from the sale of Pepsi *and* the sale of pizza) or in another restaurant (where Pepsi will profit only from the sale of the Pepsi, not the pizza). Thus, in some instances, the underlying premise in Pepsi's argument damages Pepsi rather than Coke. It wouldn't have hurt for Coke to point this out in one of its advertisements. Of course, retailers concerned with the bottom line could have figured this out without Coke's help.

Pepsi did have some decent support in the form of quotations from satisfied customers ("A few quotes," P5; "A few [more] quotes," P5a; "Pepsi is committed," P9). However, surely readers would expect Pepsi to select its testimonials with great care, and the impression that Pepsi's customers *generally* were satisfied may well require more examples. For example, in "Pepsi is committed," we hear from Craig MacDonald of Round Table Pizza. Of course, if there is no Pizza Hut near his store, that could be why he isn't worried by Pepsi's ownership of other restaurants.

Third, the themes that ran through the persuasive messages seem to favor Coke as well. Pepsi began by flaunting its success in the taste tests ("First place," P1). After Coke's "3 cold, hard facts" reply (C2), claims of the superiority of Pepsi's taste virtually disappeared. Coke, on other hand, pushed the theme of its greater sales throughout the campaign (C2, C3, C4, C5, C9, C12). Pepsi could have replied that Coke's sales lead doesn't stem from a superior product but from history, or simply the number of fountain outlets. If retailers want to give customers what they *really* want, the taste they prefer, they should sell Pepsi.

Virtually all of Coke's ads feature (C3, C4, C5, C7, C10, C11, C12, C13, C14, C15, C16) or at least mention (C1, C2, C1a/2, C8, C9) the profitability of Coke's fountain products. Service is a prominent theme in three of Coke's advertisements (C1, C6, C12). In contrast, Pepsi emphasizes service (P2, P3, P4, P5, P7, P9, P10) more than profitability (P1, P5, P6, P8, P10), although profits are at least mentioned in three other advertisements (P2, P3, P4). Given the fact that profit is presumably closest to a retailer's heart, Coke's choice of which themes to emphasize was more appropriate than Pepsi's.

The most important issue in this campaign, that Pepsi competes with its customers, was well developed by Coke. This argument first surfaced in C3, "Satisfy customers' hunger." Here Coke argues that Pepsi is competing with its own customers through its restaurant holdings. This theme is repeated in C11, "Pepsi's fishing in your pond." However, here Coke makes the prediction that Pepsi's food business will grow, emphasizing the future threat. "Competition/commitment" (C12) explicitly contrasts Pepsi's approach (competition with its customers) with Coke's approach (commitment to its customers). The ad "Beef with PepsiCo" (C13) takes the comparison one step further: Coke doesn't take money they've made from their customers and buy restaurants to compete with our customers. In yet another escalation of this theme, "Adios Pepsi" (C15) describes a pattern in which Pepsi gouges a larger share of retailers' business each year. The theme of competition is clear, yet these ads seem to build, each charge piling on, and arguably more serious than, earlier ones.

Pepsi tried to reply with its "'Mc'Coke" advertisement (P2) and the claim that one's soft drink vendor "Won't change competition" (P3), but as explained before, these arguments were not well supported. Pepsi simply reacted to Coke's charge, an argument Pepsi can't hope to win. Pepsi accepts the underlying premise of Coke's charge—that financial interests will interfere with service to customers. The problem is that Pepsi's financial interest in the restaurants it *owns* is far greater than Coke's interest in its largest customer.

Pepsi has a much better argument in its claim that experience in the restaurant business will enable it to help serve its customers' needs. This was hinted at, but not developed, in "Who's winning (P7). "Pepsi & Coke agree" (P8) did develop this position. Testimonials from satisfied customers (P5, P10) reinforced this claim. Unfortunately, Pepsi refused to abandon its weak arguments about McDonald's, returning to them in the "Driving traffic" (P8) advertisements in October and November 1991.

Thus, Coke's advertising campaign contained three key elements: sales lead, profits for its customers, and Pepsi's restaurant competition (it also mentioned its service). This created a campaign that was interesting and diverse, yet possessed several key unifying themes. Pepsi stressed service more than profits. Pepsi also gave up too easily on the taste-test advertisements ("First place," P1). Pepsi's response to Coke's attack on its competition with its own customers was in places counterproductive (allegations about McDonald's) or not persuasive (need for more testimonials).

REACTION TO COKE AND PEPSI'S MARKETING EFFORTS

Having argued that Coke's advertising campaign was generally superior to Pepsi's, I now offer evidence that Coke's advertisements were in fact more effective than Pepsi's. First, according to *Beverage Digest* figures (Konrad & DeGeorge, 1991, p. 71), while Pepsi has recently obtained new accounts buying 30 million cases of soft drinks (Bonanza, Howard Johnson, Marriot, National Amusements [movie theaters], Norwegian Cruise Lines, Sizzler), Coke secured new accounts worth 100 million cases (Burger King, Casey's, Druther's/Dairy Queen, Pizza Inn, TW Services, Wendy's). Thus, these figures suggest that Coca-Cola is obtaining new fountain business at over three times the rate of Pepsi-Cola.

Second, several franchises have recently switched from Pepsi to Coke. "Since mid-1990, Coke has wrested such major accounts from Pepsi as Burger King, Wendy's, and TW Services, a large Hardee's franchisee" (Konrad & DeGeorge, 1991, p. 71). Also switching were Casey's General Stores and Pizza Inn. So, Coke has persuaded several large companies to drop Pepsi products in favor of the Coke line.

Finally, several companies have reported that Pepsi's ownership of other food chains was a factor in the decision to switch from Pepsi to Coke. Druther's Systems, a sixty-five-restaurant chain, "switched over to Coke in April, in part because of the competition issue" (Konrad & DeGeorge, 1991, p. 71). "'Grand Met [Burger King's new owner] viewed the chain's use of Pepsi-Cola as pouring money into a competitor's pocket,' said Jesse Meyers, publisher of *Beverage Digest*...'that's the reason for the change, plain and simple'" (Carlino, 1990, p. 8). A representative from a Burger King franchise said, "I don't think we would have switched if it hadn't been for the competitive situation with Pepsi" (Konrad & DeGeorge, 1991, p. 72). Given the fact that this is a prominent feature of Coke's advertising campaign—and it is an issue Pepsi tried to turn to its advantage ("'Mc'Coke")—this evidence is consistent with the claim that Coke's advertisements were more effective than Pepsi's. While there is no direct proof that these advertisements were responsible for Coke's fountain sales success, it seems likely that they contributed to it.

IMPLICATIONS

What can we say about persuasive attack and defense from this analysis? First, Coke's persuasive messages were replete with statistics about the extent of Pepsi's investment in fast-food restaurants and their market share. Coke even had statistics (83 percent) concerning how much of the increase in traffic in Pepsi's restaurants came from other fast-food outlets. On the other hand, Pepsi offered innuendo and suspicion, extremely weak in contrast. In particular, Pepsi should never have made the charges about Coke and McDonald's in "Accounts payable/receivable" (P6) without substantiation. In short, Pepsi made indefensible attacks while Coke made powerful ones.

Does this simply mean "tell the truth in attack and defense," or offer proof for controversial and important claims? Coke had an undeniable advantage with certain facts (as presumably accepted by its audience), and it presented them effectively. However, which facts were selected for emphasis is at least as important as the facts themselves. Pepsi should not have chosen to make the charges in the "Accounts payable/receivable" message (P6) without adequate substantiation. On the other hand, Pepsi could have made much better use of the taste preference argument, as suggested earlier. It could have emphasized an argument buried in "'Mc'Coke" (P2) that only Pepsi offers local suppliers to all of its customers.

Both Coke and Pepsi denied charges from the other about concern for their customers, and both attacked their accuser. Coke's denial was forceful, delivered by a prominent spokesperson, Charles S. Frenette, senior vice president and general manager. In light of the weakness of Pepsi's charges (no concrete support), this denial was more than adequate. Pepsi's denials—especially when the strength of Coke's attacks is taken into account—were ineffectual ("Won't change competition," P3). Pepsi was on the right track with testimonials from its customers, but it needed more of them to combat the suspicion that it had selected atypical sources, and it shouldn't have run the "driving traffic" ads (P8).

Both companies employed bolstering extensively. While this undoubtedly aided both, Coke's campaign tended to emphasize profitability for its customers more than Pepsi's (Coke simply had a greater number of advertisements that featured profits than Pepsi, and the proportion of ads devoted to profits was higher in Coke's than in Pepsi's campaign). While both used bolstering, Coke's instances of bolstering may have been better designed to appeal to the audience than Pepsi's.

Coke was the only persuader to use transcendence. Pepsi's potentially powerful argument that people preferred the taste of Pepsi products (at least, they preferred Diet Pepsi to Diet Coke) was completely defused. Coke managed to shift the comparison between Pepsi products and Coke products from a criterion that favored Pepsi (taste) to one that favored Coke (sales volume).

It is worth noting that neither company used mortification. Coke had no reason to do so. However, in Frenette's "Open letter" (C8), Coke charged not only that Pepsi had published false accusations against Coke, but that Pepsi had printed the lies a second time *after* Coke had informed Pepsi of the falsehoods. While Frenette did not directly accuse Pepsi of unfair and unethical behavior, he stressed Coke's policy of "consistently dealing with all of our customers fairly, equitably, and ethically for over 105 years" (May 28, 1991, p. 25). Pepsi let this powerful attack pass without any comment. It appeared as if Pepsi was unconcerned about the impression it had created. While Pepsi should not have made such accusations without substantiation, once made, Pepsi should have apologized. Its ad copy even provides an opportunity for an apology: "we hear" McDonald's price wasn't increased (March 11, 1991, p. 34). Pepsi could have coupled mortification with defeasibility (we were misinformed) and attempted to shift the blame for the false charges to a third party or parties. As it was, they appeared unethical and unconcerned about it.

Together, these elements combined to make Coke's persuasive campaign of attack and defense against Pepsi more effective than Pepsi's campaign. Coke carefully focused on the issues that favored it. Pepsi reacted, seemingly off-balance, at times counter-productively and at other times without adequate support. While the advertisements published in *Nation's Restaurant News* are surely not the only factors in Coke's success in recent battles, they are almost certainly representative of the reasons for its victories.

Coca-Cola's advertisements in *Nation's Restaurant News* were, in general, more persuasive than Pepsi-Cola's ads, a claim borne out by sales figures. Both used denial, bolstering, and attacks on the accuser. Coke also used transcendence to reply to Pepsi's charges that its product tastes better. Coke's persuasive messages were well-supported, while Pepsi's were not. Furthermore, Pepsi made unsubstantiated charges against Coke, which Coke effectively denied. This chapter illustrates persuasive attack and defense at work in the highly competitive world of soft drinks.

SUMMARY

This essay described, analyzed, and evaluated the war of words (and images) fought by Coke and Pepsi on the battleground afforded by the trade publication *Nation's Restaurant News*. The analysis argues that Coke's attack and defense were generally more effective than Pepsi's, and empirical evidence is adduced consistent with this analysis.

Table 5.1 Coke and Pepsi Advertisements in *Nation's Restaurant News*,
1990–1992

Date	COKE	PEPSI
1990		
1/22	We don't cut the cord (C1)	First place (P1)
1/29		First place (P1)
2/5		First place (P1)
2/12		First place (P1)
2/26	3 cold hard facts (C2)	
3/2	Satisfy customer hunger (C3)	
5/7		"Mc"Coke (P2)
5/14	Deliver more than syrup (C1a/2)	
5/21		Won't change competition (P3)
6/4	Improves cash flow (C4)	
9/17	MagiCup (C5)	
10/1		Commitment you can count on (P4)
10/8	MagiCup (C5)	
10/22		A few quotes (P5)
11/12		A few quotes (P5)
11/26	Thanks to customers (C6)	
12/10	Satisfy customer hunger (C3)	
12/17	Thanks to customers (C6)	
12/17	Liquid assets = profits (C7)	A few [more] quotes (P5a)
1991		
2/11		Commitment you can count on (P4)
3/11		Accounts payable/receivable (P6)
3/25		Accounts payable/receivable (P6)

Date	COKE	PEPSI
4/28	Open letter (C8)	
4/29	Heart of the matter (C9)	
5/20	Bottom line (C10)	Who's winning (P7)
7/15	Pepsi's fishing your pond (C11)	
10/17	Bottom line (C10a)	Driving traffic (P8)
11/11	Competition/commitment (C12)	
11/18		Pepsi is committed (P9)
11/18		Driving traffic (P8)
1992		
5/11	Beef with Pepsico (C13)	Pepsi & Coke agree (P10)
5/18	Bag of money (C14)	
8/3		Pepsi & Coke agree (P10a)
8/24	Bag of money (C14a)	
9/21	Profits flow (C15)	Pepsi & Coke agree (P10a)
10/12	Bag of money (C14a)	
11/30	Profits flow (C15)	
12/21	Adios Pepsi (C16)	

6   Exxon and the *Valdez* Oil Spill

This chapter begins by discussing the background of the Exxon *Valdez* oil spill. Then, a critical analysis applies the strategies of image restoration to Exxon's discourse. Exxon's defensive efforts are evaluated and public reaction is examined to establish whether it corroborates that evaluation. Finally, implications for image restoration discourse are discussed.

BACKGROUND OF THE CONTROVERSY

On March 24, 1989, the Exxon oil tanker *Valdez* struck a reef, creating "the nation's worst oil spill," "threatening 600 miles of coastline" ("Oil Slick Spreads," 1989, p. 1). After nine days, the oil slick had "spread over an area the size of Rhode Island, more than 1,000 square miles" (Peterson, 1989, p. A17). Over ten million gallons of oil were released (Hilts, 1989, p. A6).

The effects of the oil spill were diverse but uniformly negative. President Bush declared that the oil spill was "a major tragedy both for the environment and the people up there" (Hoffman, 1989, p. A6). The petroleum compounds in the oil slick, "all of them poisonous and carcinogenic, seemed certain to enter the food chain," which "could damage wildlife as well as carrying toxic chemicals into foods consumed by people" (Browne, 1989, p. A12). The danger to the environment was expected to last at least ten years (Hilts, 1989, p. A6). Stories and pictures of oil-soaked animals filled the news. For example, the *New York Times* reported:

> On a small pebbled beach on Eleanor Island, what appeared to be
> a blackened rock turned out to be a seabird befouled with oil. As

> a helicopter descended, the frightened bird raised its wings to
> flee but was unable to lift itself into the air. Just off Seal Island, a
> large group of sea lions swam in a tight knot straining to keep
> their heads well above the oily surface. (Shabecoff, 1989a, p. A12)

Nor were environmental effects the only damage caused by the
Exxon *Valdez* oil spill. EPA official William J. Riley noted that both
the Alaskan salmon and herring industries were at risk. Harlan, Sullivan, and Barrett reported that "The wholesale spot price for gasoline has jumped more than 40 cents a gallon" since the oil spill
(1989, p. A4). Potts explained that the oil spill could also restrict
oil companies' plans for further exploration and development of
Alaskan oil (1989, p. A17). While Alaskans generally and those in
the area fishing industry specifically were most directly affected,
environmental concerns were important to an increasing number
of Americans, and the gasoline price increases hit everyone.

Thus, it should not be surprising that this incident fostered a
negative impression of Exxon. This was the worst oil spill in United
States history, and the news media made no secret of this fact. Furthermore, it seemed as if every day more bad news came out. At
first the public learned of the magnitude of the disaster and its
effects on the environment; later, attributions of responsibility
began to emerge. We learned of charges that Exxon's captain had
made bad judgments. For example, Wells indicated that "contrary
to company policy, Capt. Joseph Hazelwood ordered the Exxon
Valdez put on automatic pilot in confined water, set a potentially
risky course..., and left the ship in the hands of a relatively inexpe-
rienced third mate" (1989, p. A8). Admiral Paul Yost, Coast Guard
Commandant, explained that "It was not treacherous in the area
they went aground. It's 10 miles wide. Your children could drive a
tanker up through it" (Hoffman, 1989, p. A6).

Suspicions that Captain Hazelwood had been intoxicated also
surfaced (Jones, 1989). For a time Hazelwood's whereabouts were
unknown, leaving the public to believe that he was hiding from justice (McCoy, 1989). Complaints about the way in which Exxon
was cleaning up the oil spill also received media attention (see,
e.g., Witkin, Malcolm, & Suro, 1989). In July, a story broke concerning destruction of evidence (erasure of tapes of telephone
conversations about the oil spill and its cleanup) by Exxon (Suro,
1989). It should be clear that the huge oil spill from the supertanker *Valdez* created an extremely serious threat to Exxon's corporate image.

Exxon faced two quite different problems that developed out of the Valdez oil spill. The first and most obvious threat to Exxon's image came from the oil spill itself. However, it is arguable that the damage from the spill was not as serious as it might first appear. While this was an enormous disaster, the largest in American history, people realize that accidents do happen, and of course no one believed Exxon deliberately ran the *Valdez* into the reef. Thus, the oil spill itself may have been a manageable threat to Exxon's image.

However, once the spill happened people quite reasonably believed that Exxon had a legal and moral obligation to clean up its mess. The cleanup efforts were handled by Exxon and Alyeska Pipeline Service Company, a consortium of eight oil companies that operates the Valdez oil terminal and is responsible for reacting to oil spills. Unfortunately for Exxon's image, however, reports of the cleanup were arguably as damaging to Exxon as the oil spill itself, if not even more so.

Browne (1989) reported that "scientists . . . said Exxon had been very badly prepared to handle the disaster" (p. A12). For example, supplies on hand were inadequate: only enough dispersant was available to counteract a 6,500-barrel spill, but over 240,000 barrels had leaked into the ocean (Wells & McCoy, 1989). Alyeska had taken its barge out of service for repairs. After the spill, it was loaded with the wrong equipment (equipment for draining oil from tankers instead of booms for containing the oil spill). Astonishingly, the "first full emergency crew did not arrive at the spill site until at least 14 hours after the shipwreck" (Witkin, Malcolm, & Suro, 1989, p. A30). Even worse, arrival of the crews did not mean that the cleanup was underway. Crew members were "assigned to boats with no apparent mission. . . . They idled away the hours playing poker" (Wells & McCoy, 1989, p. A4). These reports of the inefficient and lethargic response to the disaster created new damage to Exxon's already weakened image. Even though some of these problems are attributable to Alyeska rather than Exxon, it seems unlikely that the public would use this distinction to hold Exxon blameless.

Wells and McCoy (1989) reported that the "lack of preparedness makes a mockery of a 250-page containment plan. . . . The plan, for example, required encirclement of a spill or tanker within five hours. The Exxon *Valdez* wasn't encircled for 35 hours" (p. A1). Alaska's attorney general, Douglas Baily, observed that "it does appear they could have responded more effectively, and so we have to determine whether there was a conscious decision not to respond" (Witkin, Malcolm, & Suro, 1989, p. A1). After five days, fewer than 4,000 of the 240,000 barrels spilled had been recovered, and Exxon "now admits it has lost its best chance to contain the spill" (Egan, 1989, p. 1). Wells and McCoy succinctly summed up the situations by describing the cleanup efforts as "far too little, too late" (1989, p. 1).

Accidents do happen, but it is generally assumed that those responsible will make a reasonable effort to correct the problems they have caused. Although Exxon was supposed to be prepared to clean up an accident of this nature, their response appeared completely inadequate. As could be expected, Exxon's image suffered substantially. For example, Sullivan (1989b) reported that eighteen thousand of Exxon's customers had returned their credit cards in protest over the *Valdez* oil spill. An annual stockholders' meeting found Chairman "Rawl fending off irate questions from shareholders frustrated over the company's handling of the oil spill in Alaska" (Sullivan, 1989a, p. A3). Shabecoff (1989c) revealed that six environmental and consumer groups proposed a boycott of Exxon products. Potts (1989) indicated that Exxon's "past record . . . as a company that is well-managed and generally sensitive to the environment has been tarnished by this accident . . . particularly by the perception that the company moved slowly and ineffectively to attempt to contain the spill" (p. A17). He concluded that the public impression was that "Exxon bungled the handling" of the oil spill (p. A1). This impression reached deep into the American conscious, as Exxon became the butt of jokes on David Letterman—top ten reasons given by the captain for the spill—and on *Saturday Night Live*—a spot for the Exxon Supertanker Piloting School complete with telephone number: 1-800-OIL-SPILL (Potts, 1989).

Thus, evidence suggests that Exxon's reputation was significantly threatened by the *Valdez* oil spill. While there was not a single attacker, the numerous negative media stories functioned as an attack. One essay (Williams & Treadaway, 1992) analyzes this incident as an instance of corporate crisis communication. However, that analysis focuses at a more abstract level (e.g., take a proactive stance, restore/maintain public confidence) than the analysis developed here. This chapter applies the typology of image restoration strategies to analyze Exxon's defensive discourse at a more specific level.

CRITICAL ANALYSIS OF EXXON'S IMAGE RESTORATION
DISCOURSE

Exxon's defense included three major components. First, Exxon
attempted to shift the blame for the spill to Captain Hazelwood.
Second, it tried to reduce the offensiveness of the spill (through
minimization and bolstering). Finally, it portrayed itself as correcting the causes of the problem.

Shifting the Blame

The initial problem faced by Exxon was the spill itself, and an obvious scapegoat existed here. Not only had the captain been intoxicated, but he had set a risky course and then turned the ship over
to an unqualified third mate. As soon as the government
announced results of a blood test on the captain of the *Valdez*,
Joseph Hazelwood, Exxon took action. Hazelwood "was fired
today after federal investigators reported that a blood test, taken
more than 10 1/2 hours after the tanker struck a reef, showed that
his alcohol level was well above the Coast Guard maximum for anyone in charge of such a vessel" (Mathews & Peterson, 1989, p. A1).
It was easy for the public to identify him as the proximate cause of
the disaster.

   This action may have had some positive effect on Exxon's
image. The company identified and eliminated the cause of the
problem. The "guilty party" was punished (by being fired from his
job) and rendered unable to commit the same tragic act again (by
being denied the opportunity to captain a supertanker for Exxon
in the future). However, it was reported that Exxon "admitted that
it knew the captain had gone through an alcohol detoxification
program, but still put him in command of its largest tanker" (Wells
& McCoy, 1989, p. A1). Thus, this action, while not completely
exonerating Exxon, might have helped the company's image, but
given the fact that Exxon knew of his alcohol problems and still
selected him to captain meant that Exxon still shared the blame.

   Exxon also attempted to shift the blame for the delay in cleaning up the oil, the second, and possibly more damaging threat to
its image. Lawrence Rawl, chairman of Exxon, "blamed state officials and the Coast Guard for the delay, charging...that the company could not obtain immediate authorization on the scene to
begin cleaning up the oil or applying a chemical dispersant"
(Mathews & Peterson, 1989, pp. A1–6). Rawl asserted that they

were ready to begin operations on Saturday, but "We couldn't get authority to do anything until 8:45 P.M. Sunday" ("Exxon Says," 1989, p. A12). Similarly, Lee Raymond, president of Exxon, "told ABC News yesterday that he blamed 'ultimately the Coast Guard' for delaying use of dispersants" (Wells & McCoy, 1989, p. A1). These utterances seem obviously designed to shift the blame for the inadequate cleanup away from Exxon.

It was not clear that the public would accept this attempt at scapegoating. It did not seem likely that either Alaska or the Coast Guard would block cleanup efforts. The lieutenant governor of Alaska, Stephen McAlpine, responded to Rawl's attempt to evade responsibility for the delay in cleaning up the oil by asserting that "Trying to shift the burden of the blame in this situation is something that just cannot and should not be done" ("Exxon Says," 1989, p. A12). Perhaps recognizing that this would not be very persuasive, Mathews and Peterson reported that Rawl "backed off a bit on his charges" during a later interview on the *MacNeil/Lehrer News Hour* (1989, p. A6).

Oddly enough, other, more acceptable, strategies were available but relatively ignored by Exxon. For example, Browne (1989) revealed that chemical dispersants would not work effectively at first because the wind and sea were too calm to mix the chemicals into the oil. Furthermore, he reported that the oil spill would "be likely to take considerable time to decompose because the low water temperature would inhibit both chemical and bacterial action" (1989, p. A12). Both of these factors inhibited Exxon's cleanup efforts and neither were under Exxon's control. While this might not have completely counteracted the reports of slow and ineffective cleanup efforts, emphasizing these factors as defeasibility (instead of criticizing Alaska and the Coast Guard) might have been more appealing to the public and done a better job of mitigating the damage to Exxon's image.

Incidentally, Browne (1989) reports that Exxon officials did mention the calmness of the sea and wind. However, this was probably not effective for two reasons. First, Exxon apparently spent more time and effort blaming Alaska and the Coast Guard than the sea and wind. Second, as could be expected, the news media focused its (and, consequently, the public's) attention on the charges against Alaska and the Coast Guard. Therefore, the less effective attempt to shift the blame for cleanup difficulties (to Alaska and the Coast Guard) was the prominent one.

It is important to note that the analysis developed here is not concerned with the question of whether Alaska's and/or the Coast Guard's authorizations were *in fact* delayed. Rather, this analysis concerns the decision to make these accusations (and apparently to emphasize them in interviews) and the effect of these particular accusations on Exxon's image. It doesn't seem likely that the public would be sympathetic to attempts by Exxon—responsible for the nation's largest oil spill—to blame others for problems in the cleanup. Furthermore, the targets could challenge this attempt to shift the blame, and in fact a spokesperson for Alaska explicitly rejected this attempt to shift the blame. However, the wind, sea, and temperature couldn't object to attempts to identify them as factors creating cleanup difficulties, making them more attractive targets for reducing responsibility.

Minimization

Exxon's first statement indicated that it "did not expect major environmental damage as a result of the spill" (Shabecoff, 1989b, p. 42), attempting to minimize damage from the beginning. As the effects became more clear, the strategy of minimization continued. David Ranseur, spokesperson for the Alaska governor's office, declared that "Exxon's gone out of its way to minimize the effects of the spill, by understating the number of animals killed and miles of beaches affected" (Baker, 1989, p. 8). More specifically, according to Baker, "On May 19, when Alaska retrieved corpses of tens of thousands of sea birds, hundreds of otters, and dozens of bald eagles, an Exxon official told National Public Radio that Exxon counted just 300 birds and 70 otters" (1989, p. 8). Nor is this the only instance of this defensive strategy. At the Exxon stockholders' meeting, "Mr. Rawl continued to talk of the 'good news' of a record salmon catch in Alaska, even after a Valdez fisherman pointed out that those salmon were not from the spill area" (1989, p. 8). Hence, Exxon adopted a strategy of attempting to minimize the apparent damage from the oil spill.

This strategy probably had little positive effect on Exxon's reputation. Coverage of the "nation's worst oil spill" including pictures and description of damage to wildlife (and increases in gas prices) probably did not go unnoticed by the public. Thus, this strategy probably did little to improve Exxon's image. In fact, if people decided that Exxon was attempting to understate the damage, this strategy could have had a detrimental effect on Exxon's image.

Bolstering

The most visible attempt to bolster Exxon's image came on April 3, when it published a full-page "Open Letter to the Public" from its chairman, Rawl, in several newspapers (1989). The advertisement contains a very short statement (barely 170 words) that makes four points, three of which appear designed to bolster the image of the company (the remaining strategy will be discussed later). First, he praises Exxon's actions: "Exxon has moved swiftly and competently to minimize the effect this oil will have on the environment, fish, and other wildlife. Furthermore, . . . we have already committed several hundred people to work on the cleanup." Second, he asserts that "since March 24, the accident has been receiving our full attention and will continue to do so." Third, he expresses sorrow and states that "We at Exxon are especially sympathetic to the residents of Valdez and the people of the State of Alaska." The attempt to bolster Exxon's image seems obvious in these utterances.

If these statements were accepted by the public, Exxon's image would be rehabilitated to some extent. He portrays Exxon's actions as "swift" and "competent." He describes their commitment of hundreds of people to rectify the problem. He asserts that Exxon's "full attention" has been devoted to this tragedy. Finally, by expressing sorrow and sympathy he characterizes the company and its executives as caring and concerned.

However, it is unlikely that this statement substantially improved Exxon's image. It is folk wisdom that "actions speak louder than words." Consider the claim that Exxon's cleanup efforts were swift and competent. Evidence reaching the public from noncompany sources dramatically denies these assertions, revealing that its actions were neither swift nor competent. A full emergency crew did not arrive on the scene for fourteen hours. When they arrived, they had nothing to do but play poker as the oil spread. Despite plans to contain spills in five hours, this one was not contained for thirty-five hours. After five days, less than 2 percent (4,000 of 240,000 barrels) of the oil had been collected. The available evidence directly contradicts Rawl's attempts to bolster the company's image. Furthermore, if people believe the company is not being honest about the nature of its cleanup effort, this could easily cast doubt on all statements made by Exxon.

The newspaper advertisement also states that "since March 24, the accident has been receiving our full attention." However, Rawl did not publicly appear to take an interest in this case for some time. "It was not until March 30, six days after the accident, that Mr. Rawl made his first comments about the incident. He finally went to Alaska on April 14, three weeks after the event" (Holusha, 1989, p. D4). In fact, Holusha argues that Rawl's biggest error was to send "a succession of lower-ranking executives to Alaska to deal with the spill instead of going there himself and taking control of the situation in a forceful, highly visible way." Furthermore, "Top Exxon executives declined to comment for almost a week after the spill, increasing the impression of a company that was not responding vigorously" (Holusha, 1989, p. D4). These actions do not convey an image of a concerned and caring management. Thus, while apparently designed to bolster the company's image, the newspaper ad seemed doomed to failure by public perception of Exxon's actions.

Corrective Action

In the full-page newspaper advertisement, Chairman Rawl promises that "We also will meet our obligations to all those who have suffered damages from the spill." This statement asserts that Exxon will take those actions necessary to repair the damage it caused. This sounds good as far as it goes, but it is exceptionally vague (it is possible that legal considerations prevented Rawl from making specific promises). If cleaning up the oil is one of those "obligations"—and it is difficult to imagine a more reasonable interpretation of this vague phrase—Exxon did not appear to be meeting them very well.

One specific action was discussed at the stockholders' meeting. Rawl announced that random alcohol and drug testing would begin at Exxon soon (Sullivan, 1989a, p. A3). It is not clear that this corrective action was publicized widely. Furthermore, it is not clear that this program would actually be successful in avoiding future accidents. Certainly if Exxon's audience used the relatively well-publicized cleanup delays as an indication of the efficacy of this corrective action, it would not appear very effective.

Thus, Exxon's defense employed four image restoration strategies. First, there was an attempt to shift the blame (for the spill, to Captain Hazelwood; for the delayed cleanup, to the state of Alaska and the Coast Guard). Exxon tried to minimize the amount of damage from the spill and to bolster its image. Finally, Exxon promised corrective action. Oddly enough, the potentially effective strategy of defeasibility was largely ignored in Exxon's discourse.

EVALUATION OF EXXON'S IMAGE RESTORATION DISCOURSE

Exxon's attempt to restore its image does not appear to be particularly successful. Exxon executives probably wince each time a television news commentator or newspaper article makes a comparison like "the allegedly deliberately released oil spill in the Middle East was even bigger than the Exxon disaster." Shifting the blame may have moved part of the responsibility for the spill itself from Exxon to Hazelwood—although Exxon was responsible for hiring him and overseeing his work as captain—but the attempts to blame the state of Alaska and the Coast Guard for delays in the cleanup were not very impressive. The news coverage of the nation's worst oil spill probably vitiated ill-considered attempts to minimize the problem. Attempts at bolstering were ineffective, contradicted by the company's apparent lack of concern (appearing to ignore the problem for almost a week) and the ineffectual cleanup. Promises of corrective action were extremely vague and undermined by the ineffectual cleanup efforts. Thus, Exxon's reputation suffered from the *Valdez* oil spill, and its attempts to restore it in the short term appear ineffective.

The public opinion poll data presented earlier supports the conclusion that Exxon's defense of its image was ineffectual. Its attempts to shift the blame were generally ineffective, because most people thought Exxon was guilty (83 percent). The fact that two-thirds of the people (66 percent) believed Exxon had not done a good job cooperating with government agencies suggests that its attempt to shift the blame for the coverup had not been persuasive. Exxon's claims that it "moved swiftly and competently" to take corrective action were apparently rejected, because most people surveyed (77 percent) thought it had not done all it could to clean up the spill. Clearly, the "Open Letter" was not well designed for restoring Exxon's image with the public.

PUBLIC REACTION TO EXXON'S DEFENSE

Kelburn indicates that most people were aware of the Exxon *Valdez* oil spill. In fact, 68 percent reported that they had followed the events closely (29 percent fairly closely; only 3 percent not too closely) (1989, p. 1). Harris Poll data (1989) indicates that 84 percent of those polled thought the oil spill's impact on the environment was very serious, while only 2 percent thought it was not very serious. Thus, a large segment of the public was aware of this threat to Exxon's reputation and considered it a serious problem.

Public opinion data support the claim that Exxon's image was damaged. First, evidence suggests that Exxon was held responsible for the initial spill. A Buskin Associates poll indicates that Exxon was considered guilty for the Alaskan oil spill by 83 percent; only 8 percent indicated that the company was not guilty (1989, p. 2). The cleanup effort was not viewed positively. More people gave negative than positive marks for taking the blame for the oil spill (52 to 46 percent) (Harris, 1989). An NBC poll revealed that only 14 percent thought Exxon had done all it could to clean up the *Valdez* spill. Over three-quarters believed it could have done more (1989, p. 1). Nor was Exxon believed to have cooperated with the government in the cleanup: a greater than two to one margin thought Exxon had not done well in cooperating with government agencies to contain the damage (66 percent to 31 percent) (Harris, 1989, p. 1). The available information on the public's perception of Exxon concerning the *Valdez* oil spill indicates a generally negative reaction. Thus, public reaction is generally consistent with the evaluation presented here.

IMPLICATIONS

Perhaps one of the most important lessons to be learned from this incident is that defensive discourse cannot be expected to work miracles. The failure of Exxon's top management to take swift, highly visible, decisive, and effective action was readily apparent, especially in contrast with other, similar, tragedies. When executives fail to take swift and appropriate action, there is little persuasive discourse can do to change those impressions. In contrast, Sullivan and Bennett (1989) explained:

> Within 48 hours of the first reports of deaths from cyanide-laced Tylenol in 1982, Johnson & Johnson Chairman James Burke was fielding calls from reporters. Two days after the Bhopal chemical leak that ultimately killed thousands, Union Carbide Corp. Chairman Warren Anderson held a news conference; a day later he was

en route to India. Last year, Ashland Oil Inc. learned of the big oil
spill near Pittsburgh on a Sunday; the next Tuesday, Chairman
John R. Hall visited the site and fielded questions from journalists
and residents. Exxon Corp. hasn't been so prompt. (P. B1)

Exxon's initial inactivity did not create the impression of a company that was deeply concerned about the worst oil spill in American history. It did not create the image of a responsible company
taking swift and decisive action to remedy an accident. As mentioned earlier, Williams and Treadaway (1992) discuss this affair,
reaching generally consistent results, although their emphasis is
placed at a higher level of abstraction (e.g., proactive stance,
restore/maintain public confidence). Couple this with reports of
an inadequate cleanup effort and there is little any public relations
effort could have done to improve Exxon's image. However, when
a company's actions are fitting, defensive discourse can emphasize
and exploit them on the company's behalf.

Second, as with any persuasive message, image restoration
attempts are unlikely to succeed when the evidence available to
the audience contradicts those claims. The folk wisdom expressed
by the adage that "actions speak louder than words" undermined
the effectiveness of Exxon's attempt to bolster its image. Chairman
Rawl's declaration that "the accident has been receiving our full
attention," that "Exxon has moved swiftly and competently to minimize the effect" on the environment, or the pious statement that
"We at Exxon are especially sympathetic to residents" of the area,
are unlikely to be accepted by the audience, given the information
available in the media. Bolstering could have helped, but Exxon's
statements were not believable.

Third, it was a mistake even to try the strategies of shifting the
blame and minimization. We expect people (and, presumably, corporations) to be honest enough to confess their transgressions. We
deplore those who, after committing an error, lie about it. This
principle is illustrated in Exxon's attempt to shift the blame when
evidence (e.g., the media reports of ineffectual cleanup attempts)
contradicted its statements. Not only is the audience unlikely to
accept this strategy, but it adds insult to injury (it was bad enough
for you to have committed this offense, but then to try to blame
someone else is inexcusable). The fact that Exxon could have
reduced its apparent responsibility by stressing defeasibility (the
cold and calm sea prevented its cleanup efforts from succeeding)
compounds this error.

Fourth, shifting the blame to Captain Hazelwood was risky for two reasons. First, Exxon had selected Hazelwood to be captain—blaming him for the oil spill casts doubt on Exxon's ability to make key personnel decisions effectively. Second, Exxon admitted awareness of Hazelwood's drinking problem. Thus, at best they should be expected to share the blame with him. It is best to shift the blame to persons of factors over which one has no control—if such targets are available.

Similarly, minimization could not be expected to restore Exxon's image in the face of media reports of the extensive damage from the *Valdez* spill. As with shifting the blame, use of this strategy appears to be a refusal by Exxon to admit its mistake. Hiding behind apparent lies is only likely to reduce its credibility further, exacerbating the damage to its reputation. This refusal to accept responsibility can very likely engender resentment.

Corrective action was potentially a useful strategy. However, Exxon's ill-advised attempts to shift the blame, minimize the problem, and bolster its image with statements contradicted in the media coverage undermined its credibility so much that this strategy was unlikely to have much positive impact on its reputation. In fact, it is possible that the statement's apparently false claims of swift and competent reaction to the spill tainted other persuasive strategies.

SUMMARY

Exxon's attempt to restore its reputation after the *Valdez* oil spill was not very successful, as public opinion data suggest. Its attempt to shift the blame for the spill to Captain Hazelwood may have been partially successful. However, its attempts to shift the blame for the slow cleanup to the state of Alaska and the Coast Guard—as well as its attempts to minimize the problem and bolster its image—were contradicted by the available information. These strategies were, in this case, ill-advised, and probably provoked a negative reaction against a company unwilling to accept reasonable responsibility for its actions (or inactivity). Corrective action was a good idea, but especially after Exxon damaged its credibility by appearing to refuse to accept proper blame, was too little too late.

7   Union Carbide and the Bhopal Tragedy

This chapter analyzes Union Carbide's defensive discourse after the tragic Bhopal gas leak. First, the background of this tragedy is described. Then, the image restoration strategies are used to critically analyze Carbide's defensive utterances. This defense is evaluated, and public reaction to Carbide's disaster is assessed. Finally, implications for the theory of image restoration are discussed.

BACKGROUND OF THE CONTROVERSY

On December 3, 1984, a Union Carbide chemical plant released a cloud of poisonous gas in the town of Bhopal, India. The *New York Times* reported that over 2000 were killed and estimated that as many as 200,000 were injured in this tragedy (McFadden, 1984, p. A1). The description of this catastrophe on the front page of this newspaper was especially graphic:

> Hundreds died in their beds, most of them children and old people. . . . Thousands more awoke to a nightmare of near suffocation, blindness and chaos. Many would die later.
> By the thousands, they stumbled into the streets, choking, vomiting, sobbing burning tears, joining human stampedes fleeing the torment of mist that seemed to float everywhere. Some were run down by automobiles and trucks in the panic. Others fell, unable to go on, and died in the gutters. (1984, p. A1)

The human cost of this industrial accident was terrible, and its status as "front page news" assured that people would learn of it. For example, a Harris poll reported that, while ordinarily only about 20

133

percent of the public can identify a company the size of Union Carbide, 47 percent readily identified the company involved in this catastrophe (1984, p. 40). The fact that this tragedy occurred in another country arguably makes this figure even more remarkable. Nor has this controversy subsided over time, because the Indian government charged Union Carbide Chairman Warren M. Anderson with homicide and initiated extradition proceedings against him ("Union Carbide Executive," 1992).

Union Carbide's reaction began when Anderson, chairman of Union Carbide, visited Bhopal on December 8, five days after tragedy struck. Surprisingly, Anderson and two top Indian executives were arrested upon his arrival, "charged with criminal conspiracy in connection with the insecticide plant gas leak that killed an estimated 2,100 people and injured tens of thousands" ("Indians Arrest," 1984, p. 1). In an official statement, Mr. Singh, Chief Minister, declared that "we are convinced on the basis of facts already available that each one of them has constructive and criminal liability for the events that have led to the great tragedy in the Union Carbide plant at Bhopal" (p. A7). Not only was Union Carbide linked with thousands of deaths and hundreds of thousands of injuries in the newspapers, but the Indian government had arrested the company's chairman and charged him with criminal conspiracy. The threat to Union Carbide's reputation was direct and serious, demanding a rhetorical response to restore its image. On December 10, 1984, a week after the tragedy occurred (and two days after the arrests), Union Carbide released an official statement about the Bhopal tragedy. This chapter critically analyzes Union Carbide's discourse concerning the Bhopal tragedy. (For a broader examination of the Bhopal tragedy, see Ice, 1991.)

CRITICAL ANALYSIS OF UNION CARBIDE'S IMAGE RESTORATION DISCOURSE

Union Carbide's defense can be divided roughly into four parts. The beginning develops a context for interpreting its behavior, expressing shock over the tragedy, shifting the blame for lack of information, and postponing the question of compensation. Second, it details four actions taken to alleviate the suffering. Third, it describes Carbide's role in the investigations. The defense ends by expressing sympathy and hope for an end to the suffering. Analysis of Carbide's official statement reveals that it employs two primary image restoration strategies—bolstering and corrective action—and two relatively minor strategies, shifting the blame and differentiation. Each will be discussed separately in this section.

Bolstering

The Union Carbide statement begins by declaring that "The Bhopal tragedy has shocked the entire management and the employees of the company" (1984, p. A8). This statement serves to bolster the company's image by depicting it as an organization comprised of caring and concerned people, not callous, unfeeling persons. Somewhat more subtly it functions to deny that the company was responsible for the tragedy. "Shocked" implies surprise, suggesting that the company was not expecting this disaster. Had there been a conspiracy, if the company had been aware of the potential for this tragedy, it would not have been very shocking to them.

Union Carbide promises "full cooperation to the technical teams deputed by the authorities to investigate the causes which led to this tragedy." This functions to bolster its image as an innocent party, with nothing to hide from investigators. Union Carbide's report that "investigations are also underway by a technical team from the U.S.A." reinforces this impression.

The closing section of Union Carbide's statement expresses "sincere condolences to the families of the deceased and sympathies to those who have suffered." This continues to portray the company as concerned with the welfare of the victims. It ends by conveying its hopes that "the suffering caused by this tragedy shall be mitigated as early as is humanly possible." This, too, functions to create a favorable image of the company.

Attempts to bolster its image by depicting the company as a group of caring individuals frame the statement, appearing in both the opening and closing remarks. The management and employees were shocked by the tragedy; the company offers "condolences" and "sympathies" to the victims. The final instance of bolstering in this message occurs as a result of its attitude of cooperation with the investigations.

It should be noted that Anderson's decision to visit Bhopal quickly was a highly visible and dramatic gesture on Union Carbide's part, consistent with this statement's use of bolstering. This action vividly demonstrates his concern. Although his treatment by the Indian authorities might have weakened this attempt at bolstering by suggesting that they were at fault, it is also possible that the arrests evoked some sympathy (He came over to India, rather than ignoring the tragedy, and the Indian government responded to this show of concern by throwing him in jail).

Corrective Action

Next, Union Carbide's statement describes corrective action taken to help remedy the problem. These actions demonstrate its willingness to help the victims of the disaster, functioning to reinforce attempts to bolster its image. Four specific actions are described: contribution to the relief fund, establishment of an orphanage, provision of medical supplies, and provision of medical assistance.

The first action taken in response to this tragedy is "to make a contribution of 10 million rupees [approximately $830,000] to the...relief fund to assist in the treatment and rehabilitation of those who have suffered injury." The fact that this is voluntary (rather than, for example, court ordered) strengthens this form of action, distinguishing it from compensation. While "compensation" may imply guilt, a voluntary "contribution" contributes to a favorable impression of the company.

Second, "arrangements have also been made to shortly open an orphanage at Bhopal." Many of the victims were children, and while the public would feel outrage at the death or suffering of any innocent victim, this outrage is intensified whenever children are involved. Thus, Union Carbide indicates its willingness to help not only victims in general (with its donation to the relief fund) but to help children particularly with its orphanage.

Medical supplies are desperately needed in a tragedy of this nature. The third action Union Carbide announces is its "arrangements to rush in medical supplies, including hydrocortisone, respirators, oxygen regulators, etc. to Bhopal." This is another useful form of voluntary assistance, attempting to correct the problem.

The fourth action taken is to provide medical personnel as well as medical supplies. "The company has arranged to bring in eminent experts from overseas for chest and eye physiology." Reinhold indicated that "The chief acute effects of the highly corrosive gas are lung and eye damage, and thousands remain hospitalized" (1984, p. A8). Provision of medical personnel, especially those in these specialties, will help make certain that the medical supplies are put to intended use in aiding the victims.

This statement describes several actions taken to correct the problem. Union Carbide voluntarily gave a donation of 10 million rupees, established an orphanage, delivered medical supplies, and provided medical personnel to help the victims of the tragedy. Carbide's willingness to undertake corrective action is clearly designed to improve its damaged image.

Shifting the Blame

The statement also explains that "It is regrettable that, owing to certain unexpected developments which took place in the last few days, there has been some delay in giving information to the press and the public." This expression of regret again bolsters the company's image, undercutting any impression that the company deliberately withheld information. The "unexpected developments" is surely a not-so-veiled reference to the arrest of Chairman Anderson (and two top Indian executives) upon his arrival in Bhopal. This statement functions to shift the blame for the delay in providing a public statement from Union Carbide to the source of those unexpected developments. No attempt is made in the statement to shift the blame for the tragedy itself, though.

Differentiation

The statement brings up the matter of compensation, recognizing that this is a complex issue. Reinforcing the company's image by indicating its desire for a speedy resolution, Union Carbide declares that "it is hoped that it [compensation] can be decided upon as soon as possible." Postponing the issue of compensation helps avoid the stigma of guilt that accompanies payment of compensation. Innocent parties may *volunteer aid* to help the injured, but only the guilty give *compensation* to victims.

Therefore, this discourse by Union Carbide attempted to restore its image after the disastrous Bhopal gas leak. It relied primarily on the strategies of bolstering and corrective action, but included relatively minor attempts to shift the blame and differentiate.

EVALUATION OF UNION CARBIDE'S IMAGE RESTORATION DISCOURSE

It appears important for a person or company at fault to admit this immediately and accept responsibility for undesirable actions. Initially denying and then accepting blame can damage credibility. It appeared that Union Carbide was clearly responsible for the deaths and injuries. However, the statement analyzed here does not accept responsibility for the tragedy or apologize for the deaths and injuries. It might have been possible, for example, to have shifted the blame to faulty equipment (which could lead directly into plans to prevent recurrence of the problem, another missing element, discussed below).

In fairness to Union Carbide, such statements may have been considered inappropriate because of potential litigation (lawyers may have advised against public admissions of responsibility before legal action had been settled). Nevertheless, the fact that such statements were not made, regardless of the reason for the omission, was surely detrimental to Carbide's image restoration efforts.

Carbide did take corrective action, and these moves were emphasized in its defensive statement. Money was donated to victims of the tragedy, medical supplies were delivered, medical personnel were sent, and an orphanage was established. All of these steps functioned to alleviate the suffering and were appropriate image restoration efforts. However, two factors combined to undermine the effectiveness of this strategy in Carbide's image defense.

First, the statement made no effort to assure people that this sort of tragedy would not recur. Again, this may have been omitted on the advice of Union Carbide's attorneys, on the assumption that discussion of steps taken to prevent future leaks may be used against it in courts as evidence of Carbide's culpability. Still, the strategy of taking corrective action would have been more persuasive if steps announced to avoid future leaks had been emphasized in the defensive statement. While the victims of the terrible accident needed help, what happened once could happen again, and people would naturally want reassurances that this tragedy would not be repeated.

Second, the statement's use of differentiation concerning one corrective action (the money we donated was *not* compensation for injury we inflicted; it is simply a voluntary contribution) had drawbacks. While it is desirable to help the victims of the tragedy, the use of differentiation here had the effect of reinforcing Carbide's refusal to accept responsibility for its actions. Inclusion of this strategy may have helped Carbide's image, but if it did, the effectiveness of this appeal was surely limited.

Furthermore, Union Carbide's use of shifting the blame was likely to be ineffectual. Given the fact that the most serious concerns surely were over the cause of the tragedy itself (not over any delay in Carbide's discussion of it), shifting the blame for delay in discussing the tragedy cannot be expected to substantially improve its image. However, it does not appear to have been a major component of Carbide's image restoration efforts.

However, this does not mean that the defensive discourse was poorly conceived throughout. This statement provides an interesting example of how image restoration strategies can reinforce one another. Carbide's instantiation of bolstering portrayed the company as concerned for the victims of the tragedy. Its use of corrective action reinforced this image. Not only did the four actions (making voluntary contributions, establishing an orphanage, sending medical supplies, and providing medical personnel) help to alleviate the effects of the tragedy, they also corroborated the impression that was promoted through attempts at bolstering. These steps are clearly the actions of a concerned, not a callous, company. Hence, the various image restoration strategies may work together.

PUBLIC REACTION TO UNION CARBIDE'S
IMAGE RESTORATION EFFORTS

Reaction to this message was not overwhelmingly positive. A Harris poll (1984) indicated that only 18 percent put the blame on Indian employees or the Indian government; most held Union Carbide's management (American or Indian or both) responsible. The company received negative marks on whether they told the truth about the Bhopal tragedy (36 percent favorable, 44 percent unfavorable). The public was nearly split on the questions of whether Carbide had provided adequate medical relief (38 percent favorable, 37 percent unfavorable) and Carbide's willingness to compensate victims (37 percent favorable, 39 percent unfavorable). Almost half stated that there was a possibility that a similar problem could occur at Carbide's West Virginia plant (1984, p. 40). Thus, this statement does not appear to have been very successful with most of the public in creating a favorable image of Union Carbide in connection with the Bhopal leak. However, despite these negative response regarding the Bhopal gas leak, more people had a positive than a negative overall reaction to Union Carbide (48 percent favorable, 41 percent unfavorable).

The unusual aspect of Carbide's public image is the fact that the public believed Union Carbide was responsible for Bhopal and had not told the truth about it—yet had a generally favorable overall opinion about the company. This may reflect a partial lack of interest in events that occurred in distant lands and suggests that salience of the accusations to the audience is an important factor in image restoration. Support for this conjecture can be found in the public reaction to a much less serious leak that occurred in a Union Carbide plant in West Virginia.

On August 11, 1985, a leak occurred at a Union Carbide plant in West Virginia. Although people were hospitalized ("Carbide a Year after Bhopal," 1985, D1), the human cost of this tragedy was far less than the leak in Bhopal. Nevertheless, Harris poll data (1985) reveal that 72 percent of those surveyed thought the West Virginia leak was very serious, and 91 percent thought that the government should crack down on such chemical companies as Union Carbide (pp. 1, 2). Thus, an important factor in image restoration, not surprisingly, seems to be how important or relevant the unfavorable event is perceived by the audience.* This may well explain why the public generally held Union Carbide responsible for the Bhopal leak, tended to think it hadn't told the truth about Bhopal, and had mixed feelings about medical assistance and compensation—and yet had a favorable overall impression of Union Carbide at that time (before the West Virginia leak).

IMPLICATIONS

Several implications for image restoration efforts can be derived from this analysis. First, this analysis demonstrates how the strategies may interact favorably. Carbide's description of corrective

---

*Another relevant factor is the question of how many people actually read (or heard about) this defensive statement. There is, of course, no reasonable way to answer that question. If few read this statement, we could hardly expect it to generate support in the polls. However, this study is designed to elucidate the strategies at work in Union Carbide's statement. The argument here, then, is that this statement was probably not effective for those who read it, recognizing that we don't know how many people did read it. Thus, lukewarm performance in the polls does not *prove* this statement was ill-conceived, but it certainly is consistent with that conclusion. On its face it appears designed to restore Union Carbide's image, and two reasons (definitely poor design, possibly small audience) may explain its failure.

action reinforced the impression of a concerned and caring company portrayed through its attempts to bolster. Second, in a tragedy of this magnitude, it is important to include plans to prevent the problem (it may not be enough to alleviate past injuries). Third, Union Carbide's image interests (although perhaps not its legal interests) may have been better served by an admission of guilt. This could have been accompanied by attempts to shift the blame to faulty equipment, which would have dovetailed nicely with plans to prevent future occurrence of the problem. Finally, salience of the harm to the audience is probably a factor in image restoration efforts. It appears that Union Carbide's image (in the United States) was damaged less by the tragedy in Bhopal than by a "local" gas leak in West Virginia, despite the fact that the latter had a much less serious effect.

SUMMARY

This chapter applied the theory of image restoration discourse to Union Carbide's statement on the Bhopal tragedy. Analysis revealed that Union Carbide's defense relied primarily on the rhetorical strategies of bolstering and taking corrective action. The statement emphasized the company's concern for those who were suffering from the accident. The statement also described several actions taken to help the victims (e.g., establishing an orphanage, providing medical supplies). Shifting the blame played a minor role, accounting for the lateness of the statement. Similarly, differentiation (between paying compensation, which implies guilt, and a voluntary contribution, which does not) also made a brief appearance in the statement.

However, because the public appeared to perceive that Union Carbide was at fault in this catastrophe, bolstering and corrective action were simply not sufficient to restore its image. Carbide's image probably would have been better served by admitting its responsibility for this terrible accident and firmly committing itself to preventing similar accidents in the future. Union Carbide may have been aided in this matter by an unconscious ethnocentric bias in the public. It is reasonable to assume that if this terrible tragedy had occurred here in the United States (rather than in a foreign country), its image would have suffered even more. Thus, an important factor in image restoration, not surprisingly, is salience of the accusations to the audience.

8   President Nixon's "Cambodia" Address

This application of the theory of image restoration is different from the ones reported in previous chapters. President Nixon's decision to send troops into Cambodia had not been announced until this speech. Hence, there was neither an attack on nor even public awareness of this (soon to be) controversial action. Thus, although on its surface this discourse may seem to be an instance of deliberative (or policy) rhetoric, I argue that it is better understood as an anticipatory, or preemptive, image restoration effort. In this chapter, I will discuss the background of this discourse, present a critical analysis (applying the theory of image restoration), evaluate Nixon's image restoration effort, describe public reaction to this message, and finally discuss implications for the theory of image restoration. As I explain the background of this speech, I will develop the claim that the speech can be appreciated as anticipatory image restoration.

BACKGROUND OF THE "CAMBODIA" ADDRESS

On April 30, 1970, President Richard M. Nixon announced that he had ordered military action in Cambodia. The long, drawn-out war in Southeast Asia was not popular throughout the entire country, so this apparent expansion of the war was likely to be controversial. Furthermore, the risk of damage to his image from this decision was intensified when Nixon's announcement was contrasted with his earlier statements on the war.

Consider first his speech of November 3, 1969, which announced his policy of "Vietnamization." President Nixon ex-plained to a nationwide audience that "We have adopted a plan which we

143

have worked out in cooperation with the South Vietnamese forces on an orderly timetable." Understandably, he refrained from revealing the precise timetable, which could encourage what might be an all-but-defeated enemy to hold on just a little while longer until we left. However, the president did declare that already "Our air operations have been reduced by over 20 percent," and then he went on to predict that "By December 15 over 60,000 men will have been withdrawn from South Vietnam" (1969, p. 68). Inevitably, there were skeptics, but this was a development anxiously awaited by virtually everyone. Perhaps more than on any other issue in recent history, our nation was divided on the question of whether we ought to have sent troops into Vietnam, but most people wanted the United States to end its involvement in this conflict (either "honorably" or immediately). It is not surprising to discover that over 94 percent of the mail delivered to the White House after Nixon's "Vietnamization" address supported the policy announced in it ("Nixon's Gamble," 1970). A Gallup poll conducted after his November 3, 1969 discourse found that more than a twelve-to-one ratio approved of the way President Nixon was handling the war in Vietnam (Gallup, 1972). The November speech has already received considerable attention from rhetorical critics (Campbell, 1972a, 1972b; Hill, 1972a, 1972b; Newman, 1970). However, critics have not generally recognized that it (as well as his subsequent discourse) was an important source of constraints for his rhetorical choices in later discourse.

On April 20, 1970, Nixon reported on the progress of his Vietnamization plan: "In June we announced withdrawal of 25,000 American troops; in September another 35,000 and then in December 50,000 more. These withdrawals have now been completed and as of April 15, a total of 115,500 men have returned home from Vietnam" (1971, p. 374; this figure is repeated on p. 376). Then he revealed that he was "tonight announcing plans for the withdrawal of an additional 150,000 American troops to be completed during the spring of next year. This will bring a total reduction of 265,500 men in our Armed Forces below the level that existed when we took office 15 months ago" (the 150,000 figure occurs twice on p. 375, and the 265,500 figure is rounded to a quarter of a million when it is repeated on p. 376). Thus, in mid-April of 1970, President Nixon publicly reaffirmed his November 3, 1969, commitment to further reductions in our involvement in the Vietnam war. His policy regarding a decreasing U.S. military involvement in Southeast Asia was made extremely clear.

However, on April 30, 1970, a mere ten days after his April 20 promises that our involvement in the war was winding down, the president decided to order U.S. troops into Cambodia. Since he had recently and repeatedly announced that U. S. involvement in this controversial war would soon be significantly reduced, he faced a particularly troublesome rhetorical problem: how best to announce a policy which was not only bound to be unpopular on its face, but which also dramatically contradicted his clear and recent statements on our diminished role in the Vietnam War? His image could suffer considerable damage. Further compounding these dangers was the possibility that the announcement of the Cambodia incursion would lead the public to interpret as deceptive his earlier statements about Vietnamization and a decreased U.S. role in the war, which would deal a severe blow to audience perceptions of his morality. His "Cambodia address," in addition to announcing a policy initiative, provided an opportunity to defend his image, to limit the damage from this unpopular decision.

Although Nixon's behavior was subject to criticism (widening the war in Southeast Asia by invading another country; ordering action which appeared to directly contradict previous utterances), specific charges had not been leveled at him prior to his "Cambodia" address, simply because he had not yet announced his decision to order this military offensive. Nixon was aware of the potential for criticism when he developed this address, clearly cognizant of the effect of his policy announcements upon his public image. In his *Memoirs* he discusses Henry Kissinger's second secret meeting in Paris with the North Vietnamese: "The situation had changed dramatically since . . . August, largely because my November 3, 1969 speech had strengthened my position at home. A Gallup poll at the end of January found that 65 percent of the nation approved of my handling of Vietnam" (1978, p. 445). Not only was Nixon aware of the improvement of his image from the announcement of his policy of Vietnamization, he also realized the risk of injury to his perceived character from announcing the Cambodia invasion: "The risk and danger involved were undeniably great; there was no assurance of success on the battlefield and there was the certainty of an uproar at home" (p. 450). He also writes that he "never had any illusions about the shattering effect a decision to go into Cambodia would have on public opinion at home" (p. 445). Thus, even though Nixon had not yet suffered an attack or criticism on the propriety and morality of an invasion into Cambodia (or on the consistency of his policy announcements)—after all, it had yet to be

announced—he was unquestionably aware of the potentially disastrous consequences such an announcement could hold for his
image. Previous work on *apologia* is limited to situations in which
the defensive utterance is provoked by a prior attack (see, e.g.,
Ware & Linkugel, 1973; Kruse, 1981b). Although at times unfavorable media coverage, rather than a *kategoria per se*, is considered
to be the attack (e.g., Benoit, 1988; Brock, 1988), thus far research
on image restoration has not focused on preemptive self-defense.

A second reason for considering this speech to be self-defensive is that while it has the outward form of a speech of policy,
concerning as it does a military operation, it nevertheless *functions* as a speech of self-defense. Nixon did not require the
approval of any other decision maker in order to carry out this
directive: he had authority to unilaterally order this military offensive (the Gulf of Tonkin Resolution). In short, he was not in any
ordinary sense of the term engaging in *deliberation* on this question. While he surely did not want to antagonize Congress, he simply did not need their approval for the policy he was announcing.
There is a difference between deliberating over the proper policy
and justifying a *fait accompli*. In this speech he was clearly court-
ing public opinion.

Furthermore, one reason policy statements are extremely
important is that the stances taken by politicians help define their
public images, as discussed in chapter 4. It should be clear that the
action of ordering an invasion of a sovereign nation would have
profound implications for the president's image—especially when
he had only days before promised sizable troop withdrawal.
Nixon's *Memoirs* reveal that he was aware of this, and it seems
likely that he crafted his "Cambodia address" so as to soften the
blow to his image, so that rhetorical criticism of his strategies of
self-defense should add to our understanding of this address. Theorists concerned with explicating self-defensive rhetorical criticism should be no less aware of this political fact of life than the
president.

Therefore, Nixon's "Cambodia" address is best considered a
"preemptive" or anticipatory speech of self-defense: one that
attempts to prevent or reduce the negative effects of undertaking
an unpopular policy. While it might seem odd to consider this an
instance of image restoration, since the criticism is anticipated
rather than actual, there can be little doubt that Nixon was
attempting to defend his image from expected criticism of his
actions.

CRITICAL ANALYSIS OF NIXON'S "CAMBODIA" ADDRESS

Given his clear and recent statements on troop withdrawals, he had to construct his defense carefully. Once he had decided that it was necessary to order the invasion of Cambodia, he faced two choices. First, should he reveal this military offensive to the nation, and second, should he accept responsibility for it? An invasion of another country is a difficult thing to keep under wraps for very long. It would inevitably come to light, and when it did he would have to respond not only to charges that the invasion was undesirable but also to charges that he had concealed it from the American public. It would be far better to announce it and put the best interpretation on it *before* opponents had an opportunity to level their charges.

Once a decision had been reached to reveal the directive to invade Cambodia, Nixon had to decide whether he should assume responsibility for it. He could have indicated that his military advisors had persuaded him to do it, and they may well have done so (although certain evidence suggests a lack of unanimity—see Nixon's *Memoirs*, 1978, p. 451). On the other hand, Nixon could have attempted to suggest that events in Southeast Asia had left him no choice but to invade Cambodia. Either of these alternatives would have created the impression that Nixon was not in control of the war in Southeast Asia, that he was merely reacting to the dictates of the situation or his advisors. This would have been uncharacteristic of his rhetorical style. Ling explains that Nixon "viewed himself as the central and controlling agent in situations from the Vietnam war to the dedication of a shopping mall. This strategy is advantageous for claiming credit or accepting laureates" (1977, p. 8). As will be seen later, Nixon attempted to link the invasion of Cambodia to the end of the war, and accepting responsibility for this decision would indeed allow him to accept credit for the end of the war in Vietnam (if it in fact did end the war). Whatever the reason, Nixon did not attempt to deny his relationship to the object which "repels the audience," the invasion of Cambodia. (For a general discussion of *apologia* which do not employ denial, see Kruse, 1977.)

This analysis reveals that the president's discourse on Cambodia appears to be an attempt to reduce the offensiveness of this event using three particular strategies. The address employed the image restoration strategies of bolstering, differentiation, and transcendence. The way in which President Nixon developed each of these image restoration strategies will be discussed in this section.

Bolstering

One strategy that functions to reduce the unpleasantness of Nixon's actions is bolstering. In one extended section of the address, he states that:

> In this room, Woodrow Wilson made the great decision which led to victory in World War I.
>
> Franklin Roosevelt made the decision which led to our victory in World War II.
>
> Dwight D. Eisenhower made decisions which ended the war in Korea and avoided war in the Middle East.
>
> John F. Kennedy, in his finest hour, made the great decision which removed Soviet nuclear missiles from Cuba and the western hemisphere. (1970, p. 452)

Here Nixon attempts to bolster his personal image by associating himself with others whom the audience holds in high esteem. Not only do they resemble him in that they were presidents, but they also made similar (military) decisions in that very room. He is suggesting that because earlier military campaigns originating in that room ended successfully, this one will also end favorably. Vartabedian's essay discusses this and other bolstering strategies as well (1985, pp. 375-76).

Differentiation

President Nixon also makes use of the image restoration strategy differentiation. He wants to redefine the situation so as to distinguish his *military offensive* from the context of *an invasion of another country*, which is clearly fraught with negative connotations for his audience. The president straightforwardly declares that "This is not an invasion of Cambodia. The areas in which these attacks will be launched are completely occupied by North Vietnamese forces" (1970, p. 451). Notice that he downplays the context of territorial boundaries, emphasizing instead who controls the territory. This idea appears elsewhere in the discourse as well. At one point he refers to a map displaying Vietnam and Cambodia with North Vietnamese strongholds clearly marked (in red, of course). Nixon then observes that "The sanctuaries are in red, and you will note that they are on both sides of the border" (p. 450). Here again he de-emphasizes the physical border and stresses the fact that all he is doing is ordering attacks on North Vietnamese, as we have done in the past. The implication is that this policy is not a new invasion but is simply a continuation of existing military policy employed in the war up to this point: attacks on North Vietnamese and Vietcong strongholds.

So, Nixon attempts to defend his image by differentiating his military offensive from the act of invading another country, suggesting instead that this offensive is no different in character from previous military actions against the enemy. When another country is invaded, that country's defenders are attacked and its territory is conquered. These actions were not part of Nixon's military offensive, and so this characterization of his policy seems reasonable. The image of "business as usual" blunts the expected charge that he is widening the war. Vartabedian (1985) identifies other instances of differentiation, but I do not discuss them here because it is not clear that they contribute to a defense of Nixon's image.

Transcendence

Further examination of this discourse reveals that the president attempted to place this military offensive into a much larger, more general context—in short, to transcend the anticipated charge that he was enlarging the war, and increasing U.S. involvement, by invading another country. Nixon's statements are clear enough to serve as archetypal examples of this strategy: "We take this action not for the purpose of expanding the war into Cambodia but for the purpose of ending the war in Vietnam, and winning the just peace we desire" (1970, p. 451). Elsewhere, the president attempts, ironically enough, to link his *invasion* of Cambodia with the withdrawal of troops, an argument which is oxymoronic in tenor:

> A majority of the American people, a majority of you listening to me are for the withdrawal of our forces from Vietnam. The action I have taken tonight is indispensable for the continuing success of that withdrawal program. A majority of the American people want to end the war rather than to have it drag on interminably.
>   The action I have taken tonight will serve that purpose. (P. 451)

The claim that "we must invade to withdraw" seems unusual, for one would not ordinarily argue, for example, that we must cut back on law enforcement in order to increase law and order, or recommend that a person smoke more cigarettes in order to quit smoking. However, when viewed from the perspective of his earlier statements on Vietnam, this argument not only is a self-defense strategy attempting to transcend from a specific action (the invasion) to a more general context (peace), it also functions as an attempt to reconcile apparent inconsistencies between this utterance and previous ones on Southeast Asia. He stresses the fact that "for five years neither the United States nor South Vietnam has moved against these enemy sanctuaries" (p. 450), a statement which underlines the novelty of this approach. His action is designed to begin "cleaning out major North Vietnamese and Vietcong occupied territories" (p. 451). Thus, Nixon attempts to transcend the expected charge that he is escalating the war in Southeast Asia by declaring that his directive to invade Cambodia is a new action vital to the end of the war.

EVALUATION OF NIXON'S CAMBODIA ADDRESS

Examination of the strategies of image restoration strongly suggests that this discourse was not optimally conceived to address this difficult rhetorical problem. Of course, no one could have announced an invasion of Cambodia and secured complete public support. However, it is arguable that Nixon could have done a better job of containing the damage this unpopular policy visited upon his image.

First, the arguments President Nixon developed in order to implement these strategies were not especially strong. Consider his use of bolstering. Although he may have gained some by associating himself with past, respected presidents—and he wisely stressed their military successes—it is not at all clear that this strategy is sufficient to counterbalance, or offset, his announcement of the military offensive into Cambodia. Any military offensive is likely to engender casualties, and the wider the scope of the war the more likely casualties are to increase. That these casualties would occur in such an unpopular war only intensifies the problem. These considerations mean that the attempt to bolster has considerable negative feelings to counterbalance or offset. Furthermore, the attempt to bolster his credibility through association with past presidents relies on fairly weak links: that they are all presidents and that these military decisions were all made in the same room, are not terribly strong reasons to believe that his action is a good one. The fact that these former presidents had made successful military decisions in the same room has no logical bearing on the probable outcome of Nixon's decision to invade Cambodia. That is, he gives no reason to believe that the decision to invade Cambodia has more in common with these particular presidential military decisions than, say, with Kennedy's decision to proceed with the Bay of Pigs invasion. It is easy to see the association Nixon is attempting to establish, but it is not a powerful enough link to offset the negative feelings toward the war. He should have attempted to strengthen the appearance of similarity between his military decision and their successful ones.

Nixon's attempt at differentiation was equally unimpressive. Even if the territory was controlled by the North Vietnamese and Vietcong, and despite the fact that Nixon stridently declared that it was not an invasion of Cambodia, his own map, ironically enough, unequivocally demonstrates the fact that he ordered troops to cross the border from one country into another.

Even his attempt at transcendence was not overly strong. He kept repeating that he thought this military offensive was essential for peace, but he never explained why. Of course, nationwide television is not the place for a detailed discussion of the specifics of the rationale for this decision. He could, however, have provided *some* explanation for this assertion. A CBS poll reported that more people rejected Nixon's assertion that this action would speed up the end of the war than accepted it ("Polls Find Support," 1970). The fact that this is a "new" offensive is hardly a sufficient reason for considering it essential for peace.

Ironically, Nixon's attempt to portray this offensive as "new" tends to undermine his image as a wise decision maker. He reveals that "for five years neither the United States nor South Vietnam has moved against these enemy sanctuaries," as mentioned earlier. If this action is as essential to peace as he would have his audience believe, why did he wait until now? Why did he let our soldiers—not to mention innocent civilians—continue to die without ordering this vital action? Nixon could have taken this action immediately after he took office if it was such a necessary move. Thus, even if his audience accepted his description of reality his image is likely to suffer—and even more so given the president's previous utterances on this topic. This was a defensive strategy that created potential problems without contributing much to his defense.

However, another reason can be posited for the lukewarm reception experienced by this discourse. Not only are these factors of self-defense individually weak, they are also collectively ineffectual. The descriptions Nixon provided of this military offensive are fundamentally incompatible.

The two strategies that Nixon developed most extensively in this discourse are differentiation and transcendence. While these two factors may not be inherently incompatible, the manner in which they are implemented in this speech creates inconsistent impressions. In operationalizing the strategy of differentiation, Nixon characterizes his military offensive as a *continuation of current policy* of attacking enemy strongholds. This description clashes sharply with the one created by his attempt at transcendence, where we are told that this military offensive is something *new and never attempted* by us or our allies in the past five years. This does not sound as if this offensive simply continues existing policy. Although it might be possible to construct rationalizations that justify these disparate positions, no such justification is present in the discourse. The fact that these two factors are the most extensive ones relied upon by Nixon in his self-defense compounds this difficulty, further undermining his credibility. He may have been better off admitting he was invading Cambodia to destroy enemy strongholds, stressing the novelty of his approach. Invading Cambodia was a new and different strategy, and he should have attempted to make the most of it through a better development of transcendence, instead of attempting to differentiate his military action from an invasion.

Undoubtedly, there are aspects of this speech that this approach fails to open up: this is not the only useful method for rhetorical criticism generally or for this speech particularly. However, this particular discourse—despite the fact that it does not respond to a prior attack—contains important elements of self-defense and does not deliberate in any usual sense of the term. Approaching what is on its face a policy speech from the perspective of image restoration may explain, for example, why Nixon chose to employ the somewhat unusual argument that we must invade to withdraw. This argument, if accepted, not only transcends specific charges but also helps reconcile Nixon's current speech with prior statements, thereby reducing damage to his image. Previous criticism of this speech (Gregg & Hauser, 1973), while addressing some issues which were beyond the scope of this essay, does not explain this unusual argument.

PUBLIC REACTION TO NIXON'S "CAMBODIA ADDRESS"

Public reaction to this discourse was not extremely unfavorable. College campuses rocked with peace demonstrations, leading to the death of four students at Kent State only five days after this speech ("Kent State," 1970). Two were killed at Jackson State as well. Furthermore, four hundred universities were affected by strikes, and hundreds more had classes curtailed by demonstrations following this speech ("Students Step Up Protests," 1970). A Gallup poll indicated that only 50 percent of the people approved of the president's handling of the Cambodia situation (1970, p. 6), but even this ratio is not as favorable as it might seem. First, contrast it with the greater than twelve-to-one ratio following his "Vietnamization" address scarcely six months earlier. Second, Gallup polls also reported that only 25 percent of those polled agreed with Nixon's decision to send troops into Cambodia (p. 6). Thus, as expected from the evaluation, this speech was not overwhelmingly well received.

IMPLICATIONS

This analysis offers several insights for our understanding of image restoration discourse. First, it illustrates the idea that rhetors may attempt to preempt anticipated criticism. Announcement of the military operation into Cambodia would surely precipitate a storm of criticism. However, if accepted, the image restoration strategies contained within this message could have blunted potential criticism and prevented or reduced the damage to Nixon's reputation. Even if this instance does not appear to have been successful at protecting the president's image, there is no reason why a well-conceived, preemptive self-defense couldn't succeed at attenuating or blocking criticism, protecting a rhetor's reputation. The strategies developed here can potentially be used before, as well as after, a rhetor has been attacked (see the treatment of accounts as preemptive by Sykes & Matza, 1957).

Second, this investigation provides further support for the claim that a person's actions (policies) are an important factor in a person's reputation. As discussed earlier, this speech is not in any way deliberating on the military offensive in Cambodia. That decision had already been made and, in fact, implemented. There can be no question that taking this action would (and, in point of fact, did) have serious consequences for Nixon's image. Thus, it seems unwise for those interested in image restoration discourse to declare that speeches concerned with policy are not *apologia*. Nixon's "Cambodia Address" seems to demonstrate the shortsightedness of that position. A person's actions contribute significantly to his or her reputation, and an understanding of image restoration discourse should take this fact into account.

Third, this analysis suggests that, while a rhetor has a variety of strategies available to restore (or protect) an image, some strategies may conflict. Although the strategies of differentiation and transcendence may not necessarily be contradictory, in this instance they provided inconsistent descriptions of the military offensive. When he employed differentiation, Nixon characterized his actions as continuations of past policies, but when he used transcendence, he portrayed his actions as a bold new initiative. Rhetors must be careful to develop their image restoration strategies in ways that avoid this sort of internal conflict. This is especially true when the potentially contradictory strategies are developed extensively in the discourse, as differentiation and transcendence are in this speech.

Fourth, particular image restoration strategies may be operationalized well or poorly. Differentiation seemed to offer a plausible argument (when considered apart from transcendence): we are not invading another country, but attacking the North Vietnamese and Vietcong (*not* the Cambodians) in their lairs, wherever they may have happened to build them. It seems clear that we are not actually invading or trying to conquer another country in this military offensive. Thus, this seems to be a plausible attempt to reduce or eliminate negative repercussions to Nixon's image from his policy. On the other hand, Nixon's use of bolstering to attempt to enhance his credibility through association with past presidents and their successful military efforts seemed rather ineffectual. The link he drew (decisions were made in the same room) is quite tenuous. Thus, identifying the presence of an image restoration strategy is only the beginning of the critic's task: the critic must also evaluate the probable cogency of the strategy as operationalized by the rhetor, offering an explanation of that evaluation.

SUMMARY

On November 3, 1969, President Richard M. Nixon revealed his policy of Vietnamization, announcing plans for the complete withdrawal of American ground combat troops from Vietnam. On April 20, 1970, he reported that over 100,000 men had been withdrawn and announced that another 150,000 would be withdrawn in the next year. America was stunned when, on April 30, 1970, President Nixon disclosed his directive ordering the invasion of Cambodia. Analysis of this discourse through the theory of image restoration discourse developed here demonstrates that it can profitably be viewed as a speech of self-defense as well as a deliberative address. He attempted to bolster his image by linking himself with past, respected presidents. This military offensive was differentiated from the anticipated charge that it was an invasion by portraying it as fundamentally no different from current policy of attacking enemy strongholds. An attempt to transcend this anticipated charge was based on the claim that the offensive was a new policy essential to end the war.

These strategies were individually weak, and the last two, differentiation and transcendence—which were most heavily relied upon by the president—presented apparently conflicting descriptions of reality. It is not surprising to discover that the speech was not well received. Nixon may have benefited from strong bolstering and greater reliance on transcendence instead of attempting to differentiate. Therefore, use of the genre of self-defense provides insight into the nature and effects of this important address. More importantly, this case study argues strongly for expanding the boundaries of the genre of self-defense, to include (either as species or companion genre) both defenses of policy (when they have clear implications for the character of the rhetor) and preemptive defenses.

9   Conclusion

This chapter discusses implications of the theory of image restoration discourse, based on the applications in the preceding four chapters as well as on other rhetorical criticisms of apologetic discourse. First, some observations concerning the nature of image restoration discourse are advanced, and then suggestions for using the strategies are discussed. Finally, suggestions for future work in this area are sketched.

THE NATURE OF IMAGE RESTORATION DISCOURSE

Image restoration rhetoric may take many forms. These types of discourses typically employ more than one defensive strategy. For example, Coca-Cola and Pepsi-Cola both used the strategies of denial, bolstering, and attacks on their accuser. Exxon relied on reducing offensiveness, shifting the blame, and corrective action. Union Carbide primarily employed bolstering and taking corrective action. President Nixon used bolstering, differentiation, and transcendence in his "Cambodia" speech, all forms of reducing offensiveness. The literature review in chapter 2 reveals many other combinations of image restoration strategies. Use of multiple strategies probably reflects an effort to avoid "putting all the eggs in one basket." Unless a single image restoration strategy is very likely to be particularly effective with the intended audience—and as long as multiple strategies do not appear inconsistent—use of multiple image restoration strategies is probably a wise choice.

Use of multiple strategies may be beneficial in that they reinforce one another. Union Carbide employed the image restoration strategy of recounting corrective action (through four actions:

making voluntary contributions, establishing an orphanage, providing medical supplies, and providing medical personnel). These actions reinforced Carbide's attempts to bolster its image by portraying itself as concerned for the victims. Here, Carbide's actions clearly corroborate its words. In AT&T's attempt to purify its image after the recent service outages in New York City, use of corrective action tended to bolster its image (Benoit & Brinson, 1994). Thus, these image restoration strategies should not be considered to be completely independent of, or isolated from, one another. Rather, defensive discourse often contains multiple strategies that reinforce each other. (It is also possible that particular operationalizations of strategies could interfere with each other as well.) However, while identifying individual strategies is useful, the strategies should also be seen as components of a broader defense.

Second, each particular strategy can be operationalized in different ways. For example, Union Carbide reported four different instances of corrective action (making voluntary contributions, establishing an orphanage, sending medical supplies, sending medical personnel). Each of these actions can be seen as an attempt to alleviate the effects of the tragedy. Similarly, in his statement before the Senate Judiciary Committee, Judge Clarence Thomas denied that he had sexually harassed Professor Anita Hill, and then he reinforced this denial by asserting that Hill had never complained to him about feeling harassed. He even augmented his denial again by declaring that she had never complained about sexual harassment to any of their common acquaintances (Benoit & Nill, 1993). The use of multiple instances of a particular strategy may reflect, as in the case of multiple strategies, the rhetor's desire to avoid relying on a single attempt to persuade the audience.

Third, while the image restoration discourse may occur in a short, intense clash of views (as Rosenfield [1968] suggests), there are also instances in which the rhetor develops a defensive campaign over time. The chapter on Coke and Pepsi examines three years of their advertising campaigns and suggests that some themes were developed throughout the campaign. President Nixon's Watergate defense shifted emphasis over time, as the situation facing him altered (Benoit, 1982). Similarly, President Reagan's defense against Iran-Contra allegations did not remain static (Benoit, Gullifor, & Panici, 1991). Even in the relatively brief time in which AT&T defended its image, we found several stages of its defense (Benoit & Brinson, 1994). This suggests that in some instances rhetorical critics will not obtain a complete view of the defensive campaign by examining a single discourse.

Analysis of Nixon's "Cambodia" address suggests that the theory of image restoration discourse can be applied in a wide variety of circumstances. Specifically, this speech clearly concerned policy rather than character *per se*. However, as discussed in chapter 8, issues of policy are inextricably intertwined with those of character. Furthermore, this application illustrates how a rhetor may use the strategies of image restoration to preempt (either entirely or to mitigate) anticipated accusations. Image restoration efforts may concern policy as well as character, and image restoration (or at least image management using these strategies) can even occur prior to attacks.

Thus, speeches of self-defense employ a variety of defenses. Multiple strategies may increase the chances for success, and strategies may reinforce one another. Similarly, particular strategies may be operationalized in several ways in a given discourse. This may also increase the likelihood for success. While the apologetic situation may be a short, intense clash of views, some image restoration efforts are better understood as campaigns developed over time, in which the apologist may adjust his or her defense to accommodate changing circumstances. Finally, the apologist may address concerns over policy as well as character attacks (the two can be closely intertwined) and the apologist may even attempt to preempt anticipated attacks.

SUGGESTIONS FOR IMAGE RESTORATION DISCOURSE

In this section I want to focus on suggestions for more effective image repair efforts that relate to the theory of image restoration discourse. Because image restoration rhetoric is a species (or genre) of persuasive or rhetorical discourse, suggestions for effectiveness may stem from our understanding of persuasion and rhetoric generally as well as from considerations pertaining directly to image restoration. For example, McGuckin (1968) argues that Nixon's "Checkers" speech was successful because he identified with appropriate values. Hoover (1989) argues that Blanton was unsuccessful in part because he did not appear sincere. One of the reasons posited by Harrell, Ware, and Linkugel (1975) for Nixon's failure on Watergate is lack of adequate support for his assertions. Brock (1988) chooses to evaluate President Ford's justification pardon of Nixon based on criteria derived from Ford's discourse, rather than from the perspective of a theory of *apologia*. The analysis of the cola wars in chapter 5 reveals advice applicable to persuasion generally (avoid making false claims; provide adequate support for claims; develop themes throughout a campaign; avoid arguments that may backfire). In chapter 6 I suggested that once Exxon made self-serving statements that seemed at odds with other information (their allegedly swift and competent cleanup), this may have damaged Exxon's credibility and undermined other arguments. In chapter 8 I argued that President Nixon's attempts to operationalize the strategies of differentiation and transcendence simply were not very persuasive.

The critic who tries to assess the apparent effectiveness of rhetorical choices has an obligation to identify the factors that seem to contribute to the success or failure of a discourse. No student of rhetoric could deny that these are important factors in the success of a persuasive attempt. However, in this section I want to focus on suggestions that relate more directly to the theory of image restoration. In other words, given the appearance of sincerity, reasonable evidence, sensible adaptation to the audience—in short, generally competent discourse—are some strategies preferable to others?

First, it seems desirable for a person (or company) who is at fault to admit this immediately. A person who initially denies responsibility for actions reasonably attributable to that person can suffer substantially damaged credibility when the truth emerges. The risk is that, when the truth emerges, the accused's reputation will not only be damaged by the offensive action but also by lying about responsibility for that act. For example, President Richard Nixon continually denied any knowledge of the Watergate break-in and subsequent cover-up (Benoit, 1982). He ultimately was forced to resign the presidency. Until the Tower Commission Report was issued, President Reagan continued to deny knowledge of the Iran arms sale, and his popularity declined from 63 percent to 40 percent. Only after he admitted that he had made a mistake did his reputation begin to improve (Benoit, Gullifor & Panici, 1991). Although initially attempting to shift the blame, AT&T eventually accepted responsibility for the interruption in long distance service, and this probably helped restore its image (Benoit & Brinson, 1994). Pepsi should have apologized for making false accusations against Coke. It is possible that Union Carbide should have accepted some responsibility for the gas leak and apologized for the damage (again, image restoration concerns may be at odds with legal concerns).

Consistent with these suggestions, some experimental evidence suggests that denial and shifting the blame are not considered by those who are injured by the actions to be as appropriate or effective as other potential image restoration strategies (Benoit & Drew, 1994). Therefore, those guilty of wrong-doing probably should accept the responsibility immediately and apologize. To do otherwise risks exacerbating the damage to one's reputation.

Of course, those accused of wrong-doing may, in fact, be innocent. Coca-Cola argued effectively that Pepsi's charges (that Coke's other customers subsidized McDonald's) were false. Tylenol successfully denied that it had been responsible for deaths to its customers (Benoit & Lindsey, 1987). Furthermore, in many cases there is no way for a critic or other observer to determine if, in fact, the accusations are true. Judge Clarence Thomas categorically denied Professor Anita Hill's accusations of sexual harassment—despite her firm insistence of her accusations—and managed to secure confirmation of his nomination to the Supreme Court (Benoit & Nill, 1993). Therefore, a second conclusion about the theory of image restoration discourse is that, if it can be sustained, denial can help to restore a tarnished image.

Third, at times it is possible to successfully shift the blame. Perhaps Union Carbide could have shifted the blame to faulty equipment (which could have led cleanly into plans for preventing the problem's recurrence). Tylenol successfully shifted the blame for the poisonings to an unknown person, someone insane (Benoit & Lindsey, 1987). Kennedy shifted the blame for the Chappaquiddick tragedy to the scene (Benoit, 1988; Ling, 1972). While this may have had negative ramifications for Kennedy's presidential hopes, blame for the accident and delayed reporting of it were shifted away from Kennedy. Still, shifting the blame can be an effective image restoration strategy.

However, shifting the blame cannot be viewed as a certain solution to image problems. President Nixon attempted to shift the blame for Watergate to his subordinates (Benoit, 1982). Even if he was correct that they had initiated the break-in and cover-up, he can still be viewed as ultimately responsible for Watergate, because the guilty people were handpicked by Nixon to be his key aides. Similarly, as discussed in chapter 6, Exxon attempted to shift the blame for the *Valdez* oil spill to Captain Hazelwood. The captain had been hired and given command of the *Valdez* by Exxon, so at best Exxon should have to shoulder responsibility with him (this strategy should not have been expected to succeed and appears not to have completely exonerated Exxon). Exxon had even admitted it knew of Hazelwood's drinking problem. Notice that Kennedy cannot be held responsible for the scenic elements (bridge and road construction), and Tylenol cannot be held liable for the actions of an insane person. Hence, it is important when shifting the blame to place it on someone or something clearly disassociated from the rhetor.

Furthermore, Exxon's attempt to shift the blame for delays in the cleanup to the state of Alaska and the Coast Guard was probably not accepted. This suggests that the scapegoat must not only be disassociated from the rhetor, but also must be plausibly responsible for the offensive action. As suggested in chapter 6, Exxon would have been better off to dwell on the environmental factors (cold, calm sea) that hindered the cleanup, much more plausible targets.

Fourth, it can be extremely important to report plans to correct and/or prevent recurrence of the problem. While people frequently want to know whom to blame, it is more reassuring to know that steps have been taken to eliminate or avoid future problems. A firm commitment to correct the problem—repair damage and/or prevent future problems—is an important component of image restoration discourse. This would be especially important for those who admit responsibility. For example, President Reagan announced changes in personnel and procedures to prevent future problems (Benoit, Gullifor, & Panici, 1991). Similarly, AT&T described in some detail plans for insuring reliability (Benoit & Brinson, 1994). Even those who are not guilty of wrong-doing can benefit from plans for preventing recurrence of the problem. For example, while Tylenol denied responsibility for the deaths from poisoned capsules, they introduced tamper-resistant packaging after the first incident and phased out capsules altogether after the second incident (see Benoit & Lindsey, 1987).

The strategy of "taking corrective action" discussed here has two variants. The rhetor may attempt to rectify or alleviate the effects of the problem, as Exxon attempted to clean up the oil spill and Union Carbide attempted to help victims in Bhopal. It is also possible to take action to prevent recurrence of the problem, as President Reagan did (finally) in the Iran-Contra affair (Benoit, Gullifor, & Panici, 1991), as Tylenol did after the poisonings (Benoit & Lindsey, 1987; Benson, 1988), or as AT&T did after the long distance service interruption (Benoit & Brinson, 1994). In some cases it may be difficult or impractical to correct the effects (e.g., the arms had already been sent to Iran; AT&T's customers have already suffered the inconvenience). However, the importance of preventing a recurrence of the problem cannot be overestimated. For example, as discussed in chapter 7, Union Carbide's statement recounted several actions to alleviate the suffering of victims, but remained silent on the important question of what, if anything, it had done to prevent a similar tragedy. The fact that another leak occurred later (in West Virginia) underlines the importance of this omission.

Of course, discussing corrective and/or preventive action cannot assure the success of an image restoration effort. For example, although Exxon boasted of its "swift" and "competent" actions, newspaper reports revealed that these descriptions were inaccurate at best. There is a risk that this strategy will fail—if not backfire—if one's actions clearly do not measure up to one's promises.

Fifth, minimization cannot always be expected to improve one's image. It is quite possible that Exxon's feeble efforts to minimize the amount of damage may have been counterproductive. When a person (or company) creates a real problem, we expect them to "'fess" up. Trying to make a serious problem seem trivial can be perceived as unethical, irresponsible, and inappropriate.

Sixth, the use of multiple strategies, one of the characteristics of image restoration discourse identified earlier, can be beneficial to the rhetor. Union Carbide's plans to alleviate suffering were consistent with the attempts at bolstering, portraying the company as concerned with victims of the tragedy.

However, in some cases multiple defensive strategies may not help the rhetor. In Nixon's "Cambodia" address, he used differentiation and transcendence. As suggested in chapter 8, these strategies may not be inherently inconsistent, but in this speech, they created conflicting impressions. Similarly, it is possible that in a defense extended over time (another characteristic of some image restoration attempts) the apologist's changing stance could result in charges of inconsistency.

Seventh, we must recognize that powers of persuasion—and the theory of image restoration—are limited. Given mistakes and poor choices immediately after the accident, there was little that could be done to restore Exxon's image after the *Valdez* oil spill—other than wait until most consumers had forgotten the incident. Perhaps a firm commitment to preventing similar disasters in the future would have helped more than firing Captain Hazelwood, but the reports of the inept cleanup efforts were a powerful detriment to

Exxon's image. President Nixon could not have expected the entire country to rally around his invasion of Cambodia, although he could have contained the damage more effectively.

Finally, analysis of Union Carbide's defensive discourse concerning the tragedy in Bhopal illustrates the effects of topic salience on image restoration. Despite the fact that the public generally held Union Carbide responsible for thousands of deaths in Bhopal, the (American) public still had a favorable overall opinion of the company. This is probably because events in a distant land are of relatively less importance to the audience than events in close proximity. Hence salience of the victims to the audience is probably an important factor in image restoration. The closer the audience is to the harm, the harder rhetors will probably have to work to restore their images.

Thus, several suggestions for image restoration discourse emerge from review of this work. If the rhetor is at fault, it is very risky to attempt to deny guilt. Mortification, although unpleasant, may be an important component of many image restoration efforts. However, denial can work, as Coke, Judge Thomas, and Tylenol demonstrated. Shifting the blame can be an effective strategy, but it is important to shift the blame away from the rhetor (rather than, for example, to subordinates) and onto a plausible scapegoat. Plans for corrective action—and especially for insuring that the reprehensible act does not recur—can be very important in image restoration. Minimization may be a useful strategy at times, but when the harms are obvious to the audience this may actually create negative feelings. While multiple strategies may be useful, Nixon's "Cambodia Address" revealed that they can also conflict with one another. We must have realistic expectations for what image restoration can do; it cannot be expected to work miracles, and one's actions must not contradict and undermine one's rhetoric. Finally, the image restoration rhetor must be aware of the salience of the negative act for the audience. Rhetors may have to work especially hard if the accusations are very important to the audience, or rhetors may benefit if the audience is not overly concerned with the problems. Surely other suggestions for image restoration discourse are possible and await further research.

FUTURE WORK

The theory of image restoration discourse has room for further development. First, as indicated in chapter 4, it is possible to further refine the categories of defensive strategies. The literature on accounts reviewed in chapter 3 revealed a great deal of effort expended in refining their typologies, in contrast to the theories discussed in chapter 2. For example, would it be useful to develop a typology of different methods for bolstering an image? Similarly, in chapter 4, I observed that Schonbach (1980) distinguished between accounts based on past restitution or compensation and those based on future restitution or compensation. If we find evidence that one form of compensation is more effective than the other—either generally or in certain circumstances—then there would be a good reason to further subdivide this category. Thus, I have tried to balance completeness with simplicity and clarity, but we may find that fourteen strategies are an oversimplification, and that there is need to further refine them.

Second, the theory of *apologia* has borrowed from other work before (e.g., Ware and Linkugel's [1973] appropriation of Abelson's [1959] suggestions for conflict resolution), and it might profit from utilization of some of the research on attribution theory. Fundamentally, this theory is concerned with perceptions of causality or responsibility, with the conditions under which an action is attributed internally, to the actor, or externally, to the situation (see, e.g., Jones & Davis, 1965; Kelley, 1967, 1972; Shaver, 1985). Given the analysis of the image restoration enterprise developed in chapter 4—image restoration becomes appropriate when an actor is believed to be responsible for a reprehensible act—attribution theory seems to have the potential to make a useful contribution to understanding image restoration.

Heider (1958) developed a theory of levels of responsibility for an action in an early work on attribution. This is desirable if the action is perceived favorably by significant others, but undesirable if the action is perceived unfavorably. At the level of association, "the person is held responsible for each effect that is in any way connected with him or that seems in any way to belong to him." Second, he suggests that when a person's actions are necessary for the effect—even if he or she did not intend the effects or even foresee them—this constitutes causality. Foreseeability occurs when the actor is "considered responsible, directly or indirectly, for any aftereffect he may have foreseen even though it was not a part of his own goal" (p. 113). The level of intention represents the degree of responsibility that occurs when a person intended or meant an effect to happen. Finally, justification concerns cases in which the person's motives stem from the environment. This analysis has the potential to further our understanding of the process by which accusers (and observers) decide to hold an actor responsible for an unpleasant event—which surely would be useful in understanding how to repair one's image after such accusations.

For example, if the negatively perceived behavior only occurs in certain (limited) situations, or only in the company of certain people, it may be possible to evade or reduce responsibility by suggesting that the situation (or people who are bad influences) should be blamed. Thus, apologists could argue that the behavior in question only occurred in certain situations (e.g., "I'm only late when the buses aren't running"), and hence the problem should not be considered to be truly their fault. The usefulness of attribution theory to the study of image restoration discourse is a question that deserves to be explored. (Snyder, Higgins, & Stucky [1983] offer an interesting application of principles of attribution theory in their book on excuses; see also Weiner, Amirkhan, Folkes, & Verette [1987] or Prus, [1975]).

Third, the theory of image restoration has thus far been applied to political speeches (Nixon's "Cambodia" address [chapter 8]; Reagan on Iran-Contra [Benoit, Gullifor, & Panici, 1991]; Judge Thomas' s confirmation hearing [Benoit & Nill, 1994]) and corporate discourse (Coke and Pepsi's advertisements in *Nation's Restaurant News* [chapter 5]; Exxon's *Valdez* oil spill [chapter 6]; Union Carbide and Bhopal [chapter 7]; and AT&T's service interruption [Benoit & Brinson, 1994]). It would be useful to see how well it works with image restoration attempts in other sorts of situations. For example, forensic discourse has been construed, as early as Aristotle's *Rhetoric*, as the genre of attack and defense. Clearly, the theories of *kategoria* and *apologia* and this theory of image restoration have implications for legal discourse. Similarly, electoral campaigns—and political debates in particular—are full of attack and defense, and while this theory has been applied to defenses from political actors, it hasn't yet been extended to political campaign discourse. Finally, this theory could be applied to such events as apologies from sports or religious figures or excuses from ordinary social actors (see Benoit & Hanczor, in press). While I believe this is a general theory of image restoration, there is not yet enough evidence to substantiate this claim.

Fourth, we lack a thorough understanding of accusation, reproaches, or persuasive attacks. Fisher (1970) declares that subversion (attacking an image) is one of the primary motives in discourse. McLaughlin, Cody, and Rosenstein (1983) distinguished four types of reproaches: express surprise or disgust, suggest that the target is inferior, request an account, and rebuke another person. Alberts (1989) identified five types of couples' complaints: behavior, personal characteristic, performance, complaints about complaints and undesirable personal appearance. Ryan (1982) suggests that classical stasis theory (fact, definition, quality, jurisdiction) can be used to classify *kategoria* (and his book provides numerous case studies of *kategoria*), but surely this cannot be considered to be an exhaustive analysis of this phenomenon. However, this important adjunct to the theory of image restoration has not been thoroughly developed (see Schonbach, 1990, on reproaches). A preliminary theory is sketched in Benoit and Dorries (1994).

Finally, the identity goal has two components. The one discussed here is restoration—and, in the case of Nixon's "Cambodia Address," avoidance, prevention, or limitation of damage. However, rhetors can also work to create or establish a favorable reputation. This work could be extended by focusing on rhetorical efforts to create a positive image. Again, Fisher (1970) identifies the motive of affirmation or creation of an image (and re-affirmation, which revitalizes an image) but does not articulate a theory of image creation discourse.

REFERENCES

Abadi, A. (1990). The speech act of apology in political life. *Journal of Pragmatics, 14*, 467-71.

Abelson, R. P. (1959). Modes of resolution of belief dilemmas. *Journal of Conflict Resolution, 3*, 343-52.

Admiral blasts back for inquiry accusations. (1992, September 26). *Columbia Daily Tribune*, p. 10A.

Alberts, J. K. (1988). An analysis of couples' conversational complaints. *Communication Monographs, 55*, 184-97.

———. (1989). A descriptive taxonomy of couples' complaint interactions. *Southern Speech Communication Journal, 54*, 125-43.

Allen, M. W., & Caillouet, R. H. (1994). Legitimation endeavors: Impression management strategies used by an organization in crisis. *Communication Monographs, 61*, 44-62.

Andersen, K., & Clevenger, T. (1963). A summary of experimental research in ethos. *Speech Monographs, 39*, 59-78.

Arafat says tape was doctored: PLO leader purportedly slandered Jews. (1992, February 13). *Columbia Daily Tribune*, p. 4A.

Aristotle, (1954). *The rhetoric*, trans. by W. R. Roberts. New York: Random House, Modern Library.

Arnold, C. C., & Frandsen, K. D. (1984). Conceptions of rhetoric and communication. In C. C. Arnold & J. W. Bowers (Eds.), *Handbook of rhetorical and communication theory* (pp. 3-50). Boston: Allyn & Bacon.

Austin, J. (1961). A plea for excuses. In J. D. Urmson & G. Warnock (Eds.), *Philosophical papers* (pp. 123-52). Oxford: Clarendon Press.

169

——. (1962). *How to do things with words.* London: Oxford University Press.

Baker, R. W. (1989, June 14). Critics fault Exxon's "PR campaign." *Christian Science Monitor*, p. 8.

Barringer, F. (1992, April 10). Ex-chief of United Way vows to fight accusations. *New York Times*, p. A16.

Baskerville, B. (1952). The vice-presidential candidates. *Quarterly Journal of Speech, 38,* 406–08.

Beach, W. A. (1990/1991). Avoiding ownership for alleged wrongdoings. *Research on Language and Social Interaction, 24,* 1–36.

Bell, R. A., Zahn, C. J., & Hopper, R. (1984). Disclaiming: A test of two competing views. *Communication Quarterly, 32,* 28–36.

Bennish, S. (1992, January 28). Show Me Furniture denies its ads deceived. *Columbia Daily Tribune*, p. 7B.

Benoit, W. L. (1982). Richard M. Nixon's rhetorical strategies in his public statements on Watergate. *Southern Speech Communication Journal, 47,* 192–211.

——. (1988). Senator Edward M. Kennedy and the Chappaquiddick tragedy. In H. R. Ryan (Ed.), *Oratorical encounters: Selected studies and sources of twentieth-century political accusations and apologies* (pp. 187–200). Westport, CT: Greenwood.

——. (1991a). A cognitive response analysis of source credibility. In B. Dervin & M. J. Voigt, (Eds.), *Progress in communication sciences* (vol. X, pp. 1–19). Norwood, NJ: Ablex.

——. (1991b). A revised conception of analogic rhetorical criticism. *Speaker & Gavel, 28,* 61–71.

Benoit, W. L., & Anderson, K. K. (1994). *Blending politics and entertainment: Dan Quayle verses Murphy Brown.* Unpublished manuscript.

Benoit, W. L., & Brinson, S. L. (1994). AT&T: Apologies are not enough. *Communication Quarterly, 42,* 75–88.

Benoit, W. L., & Dorries, B. (1994). *Dateline NBC's persuasive attack of Wal-Mart.* Paper presented at the meeting of the Speech Communication Association, New Orleans.

Benoit, W. L., & Drew, S. (1994). *Appropriateness and effectiveness of image restoration strategies.* Unpublished manuscript.

Benoit, W. L., Gullifor, P., & Panici, D. (1991). Reagan's discourse on the Iran-Contra affair. *Communication Studies, 42,* 272–94.

Benoit, W. L., & Hanczor, R. S. (in press). The Tonya Harding controversy: An analysis of image restoration strategies. *Communication Quarterly.*

Benoit, W. L., & Lindsey, J. J. (1987). Argument strategies: Antidote to Tylenol's poisoned image. *Journal of the American Forensic Association, 23,* 136–46.

Benoit, W. L., & Nill, D. (1993). *Judge Clarence Thomas versus Professor Anita Hill.* Unpublished manuscript.

———. (1994). *Oliver Stone's defense of JFK.* Unpublished manuscript.

Benson, J. A. (1988). Crisis revisited: An analysis of strategies used by Tylenol in the second tampering episode. *Central States Speech Journal, 39,* 49–66.

Bitzer, L. F. (1968). The rhetorical situation. *Philosophy & Rhetoric, 1,* 1–14.

Black, E. (1965). *Rhetorical criticism: A study in method.* New York: Macmillan (rpt. Madison: University of Wisconsin Press, 1978).

Blair, C. (1984). From *All the President's Men* to every man for himself: The strategies of post-Watergate apologia. *Central States Speech Journal, 35,* 250–60.

Blumstein, P. W., et al. (1974). The honoring of accounts. *American Sociological Review, 39,* 551–66.

Booth, W. C. (1974). *Modern dogma and the rhetoric of assent.* Notre Dame: University of Notre Dame Press.

Bowers, J. W., & Bradac, J. J. (1984). Contemporary problems in human communication theory. In C. C. Arnold & J. W. Bowers (Eds.), *Handbook of rhetorical and communication theory* (pp. 871–93). Boston: Allyn & Bacon.

Bowers, J. W., Ochs, D. J., & Jensen, R. J. (1993). *The rhetoric of agitation and control,* 2/e. Prospect Heights, IL: Waveland.

Brock, B. L. (1988). Gerald R. Ford encounters Richard Nixon's legacy: On amnesty and the pardon. In H. R. Ryan (Ed.), *Oratorical encounters: Selected studies and sources of twentieth-century political accusations and apologies* (pp. 227–40). Westport, CT: Greenwood.

Brown dismisses allegations. (1992, April 10). *Columbia Daily Tribune*, p. 1A.

Brown, P., & Levinson, S. (1978). Universals in language usage: Politeness phenomena. In E. Goody (Ed.), *Questions and politeness: Strategies in social interaction* (pp. 56–310). Cambridge: Cambridge University Press.

Browne, M. W. (1989, March 31). Oil on surface covers deeper threat. *New York Times*, p. A12.

Brummett, B. (1975). Presidential substance: The address of August 15, 1973. *Western Speech Communication, 39*, 249–59.

———. (1980). Symbolic form, Burkean scapegoating, and rhetorical exigency in Alioto's response to the "Zebra" murders. *Western Journal of Speech Communication, 44*, 64–73.

———. (1981). Burkean scapegoating, mortification, and transcendence in presidential campaign rhetoric. *Central States Speech Journal, 32*, 254–64.

———. (1982). Burkean transcendence and ultimate terms in rhetoric by and about James Watt. *Central States Speech Journal, 33*, 547–56.

———. (1984). Burkean comedy and tragedy, illustrated in reactions to the arrest of John DeLorean. *Central States Speech Journal, 35*, 217–27.

Burgchardt, C. R. (1988). Apology as attack: La Follette vs. Robinson on freedom of speech. In H. R. Ryan (Ed.), *Oratorical encounters: Selected studies and sources of twentieth-century political accusations and apologies* (pp. 1–17). Westport, CT: Greenwood.

Burke, K. (1968). Dramatism. In D. L. Sills (Ed.), *International encyclopedia of the social sciences* (vol. 7, pp. 445–52). New York: Macmillan and Free Press.

———. (1969). *A rhetoric of motives*. Berkeley: University of California Press.

———. (1970). *The rhetoric of religion*. Berkeley: University of California Press.

———. (1973). *The philosophy of literary form*, 3/e. Berkeley: University of California Press.

Burke, R. K. (1988). Eight Alabama clergy vs. Martin Luther King, Jr. In H. R. Ryan (Ed.), *Oratorical encounters: Selected studies* and sources of twentieth-century political accusations and apologies (pp. 175-86). Westport, CT: Greenwood.

Burkholder, R. T. (1991). Symbolic martyrdom: The ultimate apology. *Southern Communication Journal, 56,* 289-97.

Bush blames programs of '60's, '70's. (1992, May 4). *Columbia Daily Tribune,* p. 1A.

Bush dismisses official over passport searches. (1992, November 11). *Columbia Daily Tribune,* p. 4A.

Buskin Associates (1989, June). Market Research Report [American Public Opinion Index and Data].

Butler, S. D. (1972). The apologia, 1971 genre. *Southern Speech Communication Journal, 36,* 281-90.

Buttny, R. (1977). Sequence and practical reasoning in accounts episodes. *Communication Quarterly, 35,* 67-83.

———. (1985). Accounts as a reconstruction of an event's context. *Communication Monographs, 52,* 57-77.

———. (1993). *Social accountability in communication.* London: Sage.

CBS being sued over Alar report: Apple growers say livelihood harmed. (1990, November 29). *Columbia Daily Tribune,* p. 3A.

Campbell, K. K. (1972a). An exercise in the rhetoric of mythical America. *Critiques of contemporary rhetoric* (pp. 50-58). Belmont: Wadsworth.

———. (1972b). "Conventional wisdom--Traditional form": A rejoinder. *Quarterly Journal of Speech, 58,* 451-54.

———. (1983). Contemporary rhetorical criticism: Genres, analogs, and Susan B. Anthony. In J. I. Sisco (Ed.), *The Jensen lectures: Contemporary communication studies* (pp. 117-32). Tampa: University of South Florida.

Carbide a year after Bhopal. (1985, December 5). *New York Times,* p. D1.

Carlino, B. (1990, May 14). Cola wars: Burger King switches from Pepsi to Coke; cost, Pepsico's rival concepts sway decision. *Nation's Restaurant News, 24,* pp. 5, 8.

Carlton, C. (1983). The rhetoric of death: Scaffold confessions in early modern England. *Southern Communication Journal, 49,* 66-79.

Claparede, E. (1927). L'auto-justification. *Archives Psychologie, 20,* 265-98.

Clark, H. H., & Clark, E. V. (1977). *Psychology and language*. New York: Harcourt, Brace, Jovanovich.

Clark, R. A., & Delia, J. G. (1979). *Topoi* and rhetorical competence. *Quarterly Journal of Speech, 65*, 187–206.

Clymer, A. (1992, December 31). Bush criticizes press treatment of the pardons. *Columbia Daily Tribune*, p. A8.

Cody, M. J., & McLaughlin, M. L. (1985). Models for the sequential construction of accounting episodes: Situational and interactional constraints on message selection and evaluation. In R. L. Street & J. N. Capella (Eds.), *Sequence and pattern in communication behavior* (pp. 50–69). London: Edward Arnold.

———. (1990). Interpersonal accounting. In H. Giles & W. P. Robinson (Eds.), *Handbook of language and social psychology* (pp. 227–55). Chichester: John Wiley.

Collins, A. A., & Clark, J. E. (1992). Jim Wright's resignation speech: De-legitimization or redemption? *Southern Communication Journal, 58*, 67–75.

Coulmas, F. (1981). "Poison to your soul": Thanks and apologies contrastively viewed. In F. Coulmas (Ed.), *Conversational routine: Explorations in standardized communication situations and prepatterned speech* (pp. 69–91). The Hague: Mouton.

Crable, R. (1978). Ethical codes, accountability, and argumentation. *Quarterly Journal of Speech, 64*, 23–32.

Crable, R. E., & Vibbert, S. L. (1983). Argumentative stance and political faith healing: The dream will come true. *Quarterly Journal of Speech, 69*, 290–301.

Craig, R. T. (1986). Goals in discourse. In D. G. Ellis & W. A. Donohue (Eds.), *Contemporary issues in language and discourse processes* (pp. 257–73). Hillsdale, NJ: Lawrence Erlbaum.

Cupach, W. R., & Metts, S. (1990). Remedial processes in embarrassing predicaments. In J. A. Anderson (Ed.), *Communication yearbook 13* (pp. 323–52). Newbury Park: Sage.

———. (1992). The effects of type of predicament and embarrassability on remedial responses to embarrassing situations. *Communication Quarterly, 40*, 149–61.

Darby, B. W., & Schlenker, B. R. (1982). Children's reactions to apologies. *Journal of Personality and Social Psychology, 43*, 742–53.

Dionisopoulos, G. N., & Vibbert, S. L. (1988). CBS vs. Mobil Oil: Charges of creative bookkeeping in 1979. In H. R. Ryan (Ed.), *Oratorical encounters: Selected studies and sources of twentieth-century political accusations and apologies* (pp. 241-52). Westport, CT: Greenwood.

Dewey, J. (1922). *Human nature and conduct.* New York: Modern Library.

———. (1939). Theory of valuation. In O. Neurath (Ed.), *International encyclopedia of unified science*, vol. 2. Chicago: University of Chicago Press.

Ditton, J. (1977). Alibis and aliases: Some notes on the "motives" of fiddling bread salesmen. *Sociology, 11*, 233-55.

Dorgan, H. (1972). The doctrine of victorious defeat in the rhetoric of Confederate veterans. *Southern Speech Communication Journal, 38*, 119-30.

Downey, S. D. (1993). The evolution of the rhetorical genre of apologia. *Western Journal of Communication, 57*, 42-64.

Duffy, B. K. (1988). President Harry S. Truman and General Douglas MacArthur: A study of rhetorical confrontation. In H. R. Ryan (Ed.), *Oratorical encounters: Selected studies and sources of twentieth-century political accusations and apologies* (pp. 80-98). Westport, CT: Greenwood.

Edmondson, W. J. (1981). On saying you're sorry. In F. Coulmas (Ed.), *Conversational routine: Explorations in standardized communication situations and prepatterned speech* (pp. 273-88). The Hague: Mouton.

Egan, T. (1989, March 29). Fisherman and state take charge of efforts to control Alaska spill; Defensive steps taken after company fails to halt spread of slick. *New York Times*, p. 1.

Enrico, R., & Kornbluth, J. (1986). *The other guy blinked: How Pepsi won the cola wars.* Toronto: Bantam.

Exxon says cleanup authorization was late. (1989, March 31). *New York Times*, p. A12.

Farr, R. M., & Anderson, T. (1983). Beyond actor-observer differences in perspective: Extensions and applications. In M. Hewstone (Ed.), *Attribution theory: Social and functional extensions* (pp. 45-64). Oxford: Basil Blackwell.

Farrell, T. B., & Goodnight, G. T. (1981). Accidental rhetoric: The root metaphors of Three Mile Island. *Communication Monographs, 48*, 271-300.

Festinger, L. (1957). *A theory of cognitive dissonance.* Evanston, IL: Row, Peterson.

Fisher, W. R. (1970). A motive view of communication. *Quarterly Journal of Speech, 56,* 131–39.

Foss, S. K. (1984). Retooling an image: Chrysler Corporation's rhetoric of redemption. *Western Journal of Speech Communication, 48,* 75–91.

Foss, S. K., Foss, K. A., & Trapp, R. (1985). *Contemporary perspectives on rhetoric.* Prospect Heights, IL: Waveland Press.

Fotheringham, W. C. (1966). *Perspectives on persuasion.* Boston: Allyn and Bacon.

Fraser, B. (1981). On apologizing. In F. Coulmas (Ed.), *Conversational routine: Explorations in standardized communication situations and prepatterned speech* (pp. 259–71). The Hague: Mouton.

Friedenberg, R. V. (1988). Elie Wiesel vs. President Ronald Reagan: The visit to Bitburg. In H. R. Ryan (Ed.), *Oratorical encounters: Selected studies and sources of twentieth-century political accusations and apologies* (pp. 267–80). Westport, CT: Greenwood.

Gallup, G. H. (1972). *The Gallup poll: Public opinion 1935–1971.* New York: Random House. Vol. 3.

Gallup opinion index. (June 1970). *60,* p. 6.

Garrett, D. E., Bradford, J. L., Meyers, R. A., & Becker, J. (1989). Issues management and organizational accounts: An analysis of corporate responses to accusations of unethical business practices. *Journal of Business Ehtics, 8,* 507–20.

Gates admits mistakes. (1992, May 9). *Columbia Daily Tribune,* p. 12A.

Goffman, E. (1967). On face work. *Interaction ritual: Essays in face-to-face behavior* (pp. 5–45). Chicago: Aldine.

———. (1971). Remedial interchanges. *Relations in public: Microstudies of the public order* (pp. 95–187). New York: Harper & Row.

Gold, E. R. (1978). Political apologia: The ritual of self-defense. *Communication Monographs, 46,* 306–16.

Gonzales, M. H. (1992). A thousand pardons: The effectiveness of verbal remedial tactics during account episodes. *Journal of Language and Social Psychology, 11,* 133–51.

Gonzales, M. H., Manning, D. J., & Haugen, J. A. (1992). Explaining our sins: Influencing offender accounts and anticipated victim responses. *Journal of Personality and Social Psychology, 62,* 958-71.

Gonzales, M. H., Pederson, J. H., Manning, D. J., & Wetter, D. W. (1990). Pardon my gaffe: Effects of sex, status, and consequence severity on accounts. *Journal of Personality and Social Psychology, 58,* 610-21.

Gravlee, G. J. (1988). President Franklin D. Roosevelt and the "purge." In H. R. Ryan (Ed.), *Oratorical encounters: Selected studies and sources of twentieth-century political accusations and apologies* (pp. 63-77). Westport, CT: Greenwood.

Gregg, R. B. & Hauser, G. A. (1973). Richard Nixon's April 30, 1970 address on Cambodia: The "ceremony" of confrontation. *Speech Monographs, 40,* 167-81.

Groups worry about United Way funding: Fund-raising a concern with bad press. (1992, February 29). *Columbia Daily Tribune,* p. 3A.

Haapanen, L. W. (1988). Nikita S. Khrushchev vs. Dwight D. Eisenhower. In H. R. Ryan (Ed.), *Oratorical encounters: Selected studies and sources of twentieth-century political accusations and apologies* (pp. 137-52). Westport, CT: Greenwood.

Hahn, D. F., & Gustainis, J. J. (1987). Defensive tactics in presidential rhetoric: Contemporary *topoi.* In T. Windt & B. Ingola (Eds.), *Essays in presidential rhetoric* (pp. 43-75). Dubuque, IA: Kendall-Hunt.

Hale, C. L. (1987). A comparison of accounts: When is a failure not a failure? *Journal of Language and Social Psychology, 6,* 117-32.

Hall, P. M., & Hewitt, J. P. (1970). The quasi-theory of communication and the management of dissent. *Social Problems, 18,* 17-27.

Halliday, M. A. K. (1973). *Explorations in the functions of language.* London: Edward Arnold.

Hample, D. (1992). Writing mindlessly. *Communication Monographs, 59,* 315-23.

Harlan, C., Sullivan, A., & Barrett, P. M. (1989, April 3). FBI opens criminal probe of oil spill in Alaska; Exxon is accused in 4 suits. *Wall Street Journal,* p. A4.

Harrell, J., Ware, B. L., & Linkugel, W. A. (1975). Failure of apology in American politics: Nixon on Watergate. *Speech Monographs, 42*, 245–61.

Harris, L. (1984, December 31). Union Carbide's good name takes a beating. *Business Week, 2875*, 40.

———. (1985, October 10). Harris survey [*American Public Opinion Index*], pp. 104.

———. (1989, May 28). Harris Poll [American Public Opinion Index and Data].

Harvey, J. H., Weber, A. L., & Orbuch, T. L. (1990). *Interpersonal accounts: A social psychological perspective*. Cambridge, MA: Basil Blackwell.

Heider, F. (1944). Social perception and phenomenal causality. *Psychological Review, 51*, 358–74.

Heisey, D. R. (1988). President Ronald Reagan's apologia on the Iran-Contra affair. In H. R. Ryan (Ed.), *Oratorical encounters: Selected studies and sources of twentieth-century political accusations and apologies* (pp. 281–306). Westport, CT: Greenwood.

Henry, D. (1988). Senator John F. Kennedy encounters the religious question: "I am not the Catholic candidate for president." In H. R. Ryan (Ed.), *Oratorical encounters: Selected studies and sources of twentieth-century political accusations and apologies* (pp. 153–74). Westport, CT: Greenwood.

Hewitt, J. P., & Hall, P. M. (1973). Social problems, problematic situations, and quasi-theories. *American Sociological Review, 38*, 367–74.

Hewitt, J. P., & Stokes, R. (1975). Disclaimers. *American Sociological Review, 40*, 1–11.

Hill, F. (1972a). Conventional wisdom—Traditional form—The President's message of November 3, 1969. *Quarterly Journal of Speech, 58*, 167–81.

———. (1972b). Reply to professor Campbell. *Quarterly Journal of Speech, 58*, 454–60.

Hilts, P. J. (1989, March 31). Environment may show spill's effects for decade. *Washington Post*, p. A6.

Hoffman, D. (1989, March 31). Coast Guard faults ship's navigation. *Washington Post*, p. A6.

Hofstadter, R. (1965). *The paranoid style in American politics.* Chicago: University of Chicago Press.

Holloway, R. L. (1988). In the matter of J. Robert Oppenheimer. In H. R. Ryan (Ed.), *Oratorical encounters: Selected studies and sources of twentieth-century political accusations and apologies* (pp. 121-36). Westport, CT: Greenwood.

Holtgraves, T. (1989). The form and function of remedial moves: Reported use, psychological reality, and perceived effectiveness. *Journal of Language and Social Psychology, 8,* 1-16.

Holusha, J. (1989, May 21). Exxon's public-relations problem. *New York Times,* pp. D1, 4.

Hopper, R., & Morris, G. H. (1987). Symbolic action as alignment: A synthesis of rules approaches. *Research in Language and Social Interaction, 2,* 1-31.

Hoover, J. D. (1989). Big boys don't cry: The values constraint in apologia. *Southern Speech Communication Journal, 54,* 235-52.

Huxman, S. S., & Linkugel, W. A. (1988). Accusations and apologies from a general, a senator, and a priest. In H. R. Ryan (Ed.), *Oratorical encounters: Selected studies and sources of twentieth-century political accusations and apologies* (pp. 29-52). Westport, CT: Greenwood.

Ice, R. (1991). Corporate publics and rhetorical strategies: The case of Union Carbide's Bhopal crisis. *Management Communication Quarterly, 4,* 341-62.

Indians arrest and then free U.S. executive. (1984, December 8). *New York Times, 134,* pp. A1, A7.

Investigation of sex scandal hooks admirals. (1992, September 24). *Columbia Daily Tribune,* p. 12A.

Isocrates (1976). Antidosis. *Isocrates,* trans. by G. Norlin. Cambridge: Harvard University Press, Loeb Classical Library. Vol. 1.

Jackson, J. H. (1956). Clarence Darrow's "Plea in defense of himself." *Western Speech, 20,* 185-95.

Japan apologizes for sex slaves (1992, January 18). *Columbia Daily Tribune,* p. 5A.

Japanese get apology from Yeltsin. (1993, October 12). *Columbia Daily Tribune,* p. 5A.

Jensen, R. J. (1988). The media and the Catholic Church vs. Geraldine Ferraro. In H. R. Ryan (Ed.), *Oratorical encounters:*

Selected studies and sources of twentieth-century political accusations and apologies (pp. 253-66). Westport, CT: Greenwood.

Jones, E. E., & Davis, K. E. (1965). From acts to dispositions: The attribution process in person perception. In L. Berkowitz (Ed.), *Advances in experimental social psychology* (vol. 2, pp. 219-66). New York: Academic Press.

Jones, E. E., & Nisbett, R. E. (1971). The actor and the observer: Divergent perceptions of the cause of behavior. In E. E. Jones, D. E. Kanouse, H. H. Kelley, R. E. Nisbett, S. Valins, & B. Wiener (Eds.), *Attribution: Perceiving the causes of behavior* (pp. 78-94). Morristown, NJ: General Learning Press.

Jones, T. (1989, March 30). Oil skipper had alcohol on breath, officer says. *Los Angeles Times*, sect. I, p. 15.

Kahl, M. (1984). *Blind Ambition* culminates in *Lost Honor*: A comparative analysis of John Dean's apologetic strategies. *Central States Speech Journal, 35*, 239-50.

Kane, T. R., Joseph, J. M., & Tedeschi, J. T. (1977). Perceived freedom, aggression, and responsibility, and the assignment of punishment. *Journal of Social Psychology, 103*, 257-63.

Katula, R. (1975). The apology of Richard M. Nixon. *Today's Speech, 23*, 1-6.

Kelburn, D. S. (1989, November). *Times Mirror Center for the People and the Press* [American Public Opinion Index and Data].

Kellermann, K. (1992). Communication: Inherently strategic and primarily automatic. *Communication Monographs, 59*, 288-300.

Kelley, C. E. (1987). The 1984 campaign rhetoric of Representative George Hansen: A pentadic analysis. *Western Journal of Speech Communication, 51*, 204-17.

Kent State: Martyrdom that shook the country. (1970, May 15). *Time, 96*, 14.

Konrad, W., & DeGeorge, G. (1991, May 27). Sorry, no Pepsi. How 'bout a Coke? *Business Week*, pp. 71-72.

Kruse, N. W. (1977). Motivational factors in non-denial apologia. *Central States Speech Journal, 28*, 13-23.

——. (1981a). Apologia in team sport. *Quarterly Journal of Speech, 67*, 270-83.

——. (1981b). The scope of apologetic discourse: Establishing generic parameters. *Southern Speech Communication Journal, 46,* 278-91.

Laettner denies signing contract with magazine. (1992, April 17). *Columbia Daily Tribune,* p. 3B.

Lessl, T. M. (1988). The Scopes trial: "Darrow vs. Bryan" vs. "Bryan vs. Darrow." In H. R. Ryan (Ed.), *Oratorical encounters: Selected studies and sources of twentieth-century political accusations and apologies* (pp. 17-28). Westport, CT: Greenwood.

Ling, D. A. (1970). A pentadic analysis of Senator Edward Kennedy's Address to the People of Massachusetts, July 25, 1969. *Central States Speech Journal, 21,* 81-86.

——. (1977). Nixon, Watergate, and the rhetoric of agent. *Speaker and Gavel, 15,* 7-9.

Linkugel, W. A., & Razak, N. (1969). Sam Houston's speech of self-defense in the House of Representatives. *Southern Speech Journal, 34,* 263-75.

Littlejohn, S. W. (1971). A bibliography of studies related to variables of source credibility. *Bibliographic Annual in Speech Communication, 2,* 1-40.

MTV bans fire on "Beavis and Butt-head." (1993, October 14). *Columbia Daily Tribune,* p. 4A.

Maloney, M. (1955). Clarence Darrow. In M. Hochmuth, W. N. Brigance, & D. Bryant (Eds.), *A history and criticism of American public address* (vol. III, pp. 262-312). New York: Russell & Russell.

Manstead, A. S. R., & Semin, G. R. (1981). Social transgressions, social perspectives, and social emotionality. *Motivation and Emotion, 5,* 249-61.

Maslow, A. H. (1954). *Motivation and personality.* New York: Evanston.

Mathews, J., & Peterson, C. (1989, March 31). Oil tanker captain fired after failing alcohol test; Exxon blames government for cleanup delay. *Washington Post,* pp. A1, 6.

McClearey, K. E. (1983). Audience effects of apologia. *Communication Quarterly, 31,* 12-20.

McCoy, C. (1989, April 4). Captain of Exxon's oil tanker ready to face charges; pilot contacts prosecutors through an attorney; whereabouts are unclear. *Wall Street Journal,* p. A3.

McFadden, R. D. (1984, December 10). India disaster: Chronicle of a nightmare. *New York Times*, pp. A1, A6.

McFarland, C., & Ross, M. (1982). Impact of causal attributions on affective reactions to success and failure. *Journal of Personality and Social Psychology*, *43*, 937–46.

McGuckin, H. E. (1968). A value analysis of Richard Nixon's 1952 campaign-fund speech. *Southern Speech Journal*, *33*, 259–69.

McLaughlin, M. L., Cody, M. J., & French, K. (1990). Account-giving and the attribution of responsibility: Impressions of traffic offenders. In M. J. Cody & M. L. McLaughlin (Eds.), *The psychology of tactical communication* (pp. 244–67). Clevedon, England: Multilingual Matters.

McLaughlin, M. L., Cody, M. J., & O'Hair, H. D. (1983). The management of failure events: Some contextual determinants of accounting behavior. *Human Communication Research*, *9*, 208–24.

McLaughlin, M. L., Cody, M. J., & Rosenstein, N. E. (1983). Account sequences in conversations between strangers. *Communication Monographs*, *50*, 102–25.

Mehrabian, A. (1967). Substitute for apology: Manipulation of cognitions to reduce negative attitude toward self. *Psychological Reports*, *20*, 687–92.

Metts, S., & Cupach, W. R. (1989). Situational influence on the use of remedial strategies in embarrassing predicaments. *Communication Monographs*, *56*, 151–62.

Miller, C. B. (1984). Genre as social action. *Quarterly Journal of Speech*, *70*, 151–67.

Mills, C. W. (1940). Situated actions and vocabularies of motive. *American Sociological Review*, *5*, 904–13.

Modigliani, A. (1971). Embarrassment, facework, and eye contact: Testing a theory of embarrassment. *Journal of Personality and Social Psychology*, *17*, 15–24.

Morello, J. T. (1979). The public apology of a private matter: Representative Wayne Hays' address to Congress. *Speaker and Gavel*, *16*, 19–26.

Morris, G. H. (1985). The remedial episode as a negotiation of rules. In R. L. Street & J. N. Capella (Eds.), *Sequence and pattern in communicative behavior* (pp. 70–84). London: Edward Arnold.

——. (1988). Finding fault. *Journal of Language and Social Psychology, 7,* 1-25.

——. (1989). Negotiating the meaning of employees' conduct: How managers evaluate employees' accounts. *Southern Communication Journal, 54,* 185-205.

Morris, G. H., & Coursey, M. (1989). Negotiating the meaning of employees' conduct: How managers evaluate employees' accounts. *Southern Communication Journal, 54,* 185-205.

Morris, G. H., & Hopper, R. (1980). Remediation and legislation in everyday talk: How communicators achieve consensus. *Quarterly Journal of Speech, 66,* 266-74.

Morris, G. H., White, C. H., & Iltris, R. (1994). "Well, ordinarily I would, but": Reexamining the nature of accounts for problematic events. *Research on Language and Social Interaction, 27,* 123-44.

National Broadcasting Corporation. (1989, April 28). Poll [American Public Opinion Index and Data].

Navy secretary resigns position after scandal. (1992, June 27). *Columbia Daily Tribune,* p. 1A.

Nelson, J. (1984). The defense of Billie Jean King. *Western Journal of Speech Communication, 48,* 92-102.

Newell, S. E., & Stutman, R. K. (1988). The social confrontation episode. *Communication Monographs, 55,* 266-85.

Newman, R. P. (1970). Under the veneer: Nixon's Vietnam speech of November 3, 1969, *Quarterly Journal of Speech, 56,* 168-78.

Nixon, R. N. (1969, November 15). A Vietnam plan. *Vital Speeches of the Day, 36,* 66-70.

——. (1970). Cambodia: A difficult decision. *Vital Speeches of the Day, 37,* 450-52.

——. (1971). Address to the nation on progress toward peace in Vietnam. *Public papers of the Presidents of the United States: Richard Nixon. . . 1970* (pp. 373-77). Washington: United States Government Printing Office.

——. (1978). *RN: The memoirs of Richard Nixon.* New York: Grossett & Dunlap.

Nixon's gamble: Operation total victory. (1970, May 11). *Newsweek, 75,* 24.

Ohbuchi, K., Kameda, M., & Agarie, N. (1989). Apology as aggression control: Its role in mediating appraisal of and response to harm. *Journal of Personality and Social Psychology, 56*, 219–27.

Oil slick spreads toward coast: FBI begins probe. (1989, April 2). *Los Angeles Times*, Sect. I, p. 1.

Owen, M. (1983). *Apologies and remedial interchanges: A study of language use in social interaction.* Berlin: Mouton.

Packwood admits wrongdoing, says he won't resign. (1992, December 10). *Columbia Daily Tribune*, p. 4A.

Peterson, C. (1989, April 3). Coast Guard faults plans to contain spill. *Washington Post*, p. A17.

Polls find support for Asian policy. (1970, May 4). *New York Times*, 8.

Pomerantz, A. (1978). Attributions of responsibility: Blamings. *Sociology, 12*, 115–21.

Potter, J., & Wetherell, M. (1987). Accounts in sequence. *Discourse and social psychology: Beyond attitudes and behavior* (pp. 74–94). Beverly Hills: Sage.

Potts, M. (1989, May 3). Exxon confronts reputation stained by oil spill. *Washington Post*, pp. A1, 17.

Prus, R. C. (1975). Resisting designations: An extension of attribution theory into a negotiated context. *Sociological Inquiry, 45*, 3–14.

Rawl, L. G. (1989, April 3). An open letter to the public. *New York Times*, p. A12. Also printed in *Washington Post*, p. A5.

Reinhold, R. (1984, December 10). $830,000 fund is set up in India by Union Carbide. *New York Times, 134*, p. A8.

Reusch, J., & Bateson, G. (1951). *Communication: The social matrix of psychiatry.* New York: Norton.

Richards, I. A. (1936). *Philosophy of rhetoric.* New York: Oxford University Press.

Riordan, C. A., & Marlin, N. A. (1987). Some good news about some bad practices. *American Psychologist, 42*, 104–06.

Riordan, C. A., Marlin, N. A., & Gidwani, C. (1988). Accounts offered for unethical research practices: Effects on the evaluations of acts and actors. *Journal of Social Psychology, 128*, 495–505.

Riordan, C. A., Marlin, N. A., & Kellogg, R. T. (1983). The effectiveness of accounts following transgression. *Social Psychology Quarterly, 46*, 213-19.

Rogers, J. W., & Buffalo, M. D. (1974). Neutralization techniques: Toward a simplified measurement scale. *Pacific Sociological Review, 17*, 313-31.

Rosenfield, L. W. (1968). A case study in speech criticism: The Nixon-Truman analog. *Speech Monographs, 35*, 435-50.

Roth, R. P. (1991, December 27). Mayo Clinic protests University Hospital ad: Hospital apologizes, withdraws ad for changes. *Columbia Daily Tribune*, 12A.

Rothman, M. L., & Gandossy, R. P. (1982). Sad tales: The accounts of white-collar defendants and the decision to sanction. *Pacific Sociological Review, 25*, 449-73.

Rowland, R. C. (1982). The influence of purpose on fields of argument. *Journal of the American Forensic Association, 18*, 228-45.

Rowland, R. C., & Rademacher, T. (1990). The passive style of rhetorical crisis management: A case study of the Superfund controversy. *Communication Studies, 41*, 327-42.

Rueckert, W. (1963). *Kenneth Burke and the drama of human relations*, 2/e. Berkeley: University of California Press.

Ryan, H. R. (1982). *Kategoria* and *apologia*: On their rhetorical criticism as a speech set. *Quarterly Journal of Speech, 68*, 256-61.

——. (1984). Baldwin vs. Edward VIII: A case study in *kategoria* and *apologia*. *Southern Speech Communication Journal, 49*, 125-34.

——. (Ed.) (1988a). *Oratorical encounters: Selected studies and sources of twentieth-century political accusations and apologies*. Westport, CT: Greenwood.

——. (1988b). Prime Minister Stanley Baldwin vs. King Edward VIII. In H. R. Ryan (Ed.), *Oratorical encounters: Selected studies and sources of twentieth-century political accusations and apologies* (pp. 53-62). Westport, CT: Greenwood.

——. (1988c). Senator Richard M. Nixon's apology for "The fund." In H. R. Ryan (Ed.), *Oratorical encounters: Selected studies and sources of twentieth-century political accusations and apologies* (pp. 99-120). Westport, CT: Greenwood.

Sattler, W. M. (1947). Conceptions of *ethos* in ancient rhetoric. *Speech Monographs, 14,* 55-65.

Schlenker, B. R. (1980). *Impression management: The self-concept, social identity, and interpersonal relations.* Monterey, CA: Brooks/Cole.

Schlenker, F. R., & Darby, B. W. (1981). The use of apologies in social predicaments. *Social Psychology Quarterly, 44,* 271-78.

Schneider, W., & Shiffrin, R. M. (1977). Controlled and automatic human information processing: I. Detection, search, and attention. *Psychological Review, 84,* 1-66.

Schonbach, P. (1980). A category system for account phases. *European Journal of Social Psychology, 10,* 195-200.

———. (1987). Accounts of men and women for failure events: Applications of an account-phase taxonomy. In G. R. Semin & B. Krahe (Eds.), *Issues in contemporary German social psychology* (pp. 97-118). London: Sage.

———. (1990). *Account episodes: The management or escalation of conflict.* Cambridge: Cambridge University Press.

Schonbach, P., & Kleibaumhuter, P. (1990). Severity of reproach and defensiveness of accounts. In M. J. Cody & M. L. McLaughlin (Eds.), *The psychology of tactical communication* (pp. 229-43). Clevedon, England: Multilingual Matters.

Schott tries to repair reputation. (1992, December 3). *Columbia Daily Tribune,* p. 5B.

Schwartz, G. S., Kane, T. R., Joseph, J. M., & Tedeschi, J. T. (1978). The effects of post-transgression remorse on perceived aggression, attributions of intent, and level of punishment. *British Journal of Social and Clinical Psychology, 17,* 293-97.

Scott, R. L. (1980). Intentionality in the rhetorical process. In E. E. White (Ed.), *Rhetoric in transition: Studies in the nature and uses of rhetoric* (pp. 39-60). University Park: Pennsylvania State University Press.

Scott, M. H., & Lyman, S. M. (1968). Accounts. *American Sociological Review, 33,* 46-62.

Searle, J. R. (1969). *Speech acts.* Cambridge: Cambridge University Press.

Secretary of state apologizes for search. (1992, November 19). *Columbia Daily Tribune,* p. 9A.

Semin, G. R. (1981). Strictures upon strictures. *British Journal of Social Psychology, 20*, 304-06.

———. (1982). The transparency of the sinner. *European Journal of Social Psychology, 12*, 173-80.

Semin, G. R., & Manstead, A. S. R. (1981). The beholder beheld: A study of social emotionality. *European Journal of Social Psychology, 11*, 253-65.

———. (1982). The social consequences of embarrassment displays and restitution behavior. *European Journal of Social Psychology, 12*, 367-77.

———. (1983). *The accountability of conduct: A social psychological analysis*. London: Academic Press.

Shabecoff, P. (1989a, March 25). Exxon vessel hits reef, fouling water that is rich in marine life. *New York Times*, p. 42.

———. (1989b, March 31). Captain of tanker had been drinking, blood tests show; Coast Guard opens effort to determine if his license should be taken away. *New York Times*, pp. A1, 12.

———. (1989c, May 3). Six groups urge boycott of Exxon. *New York Times*, p. 17.

Sharkey, W. F., & Stafford, L. (1990). Responses to embarrassment. *Human Communication Research, 17*, 315-42.

Shaver, K. G. (1985). *The attribution of blame: Causality, responsibility, and blameworthiness*. New York: Springer-Verlag.

Shields, N. M. (1979). Accounts and other interpersonal strategies in a credibility detracting context. *Pacific Sociological Review, 22*, 255-72.

Shiffrin, R. M., & Schneider, W. (1977). Controlled and automatic human information processing: II. Perceptual learning, automatic attending, and a general theory. *Psychological Review, 84*, 127-90.

Short, B. (1987). Comic book apologia: The "paranoid" rhetoric of Congressman George Hansen. *Western Journal of Speech Communication, 51*, 189-203.

Smith, C. A. (1988). President Richard M. Nixon and the watergate scandal. In H. R. Ryan (Ed.), *Oratorical encounters: Selected studies and sources of twentieth-century political accusations and apologies* (pp. 201-26). Westport, CT: Greenwood.

Snyder, C. R., & Higgins, R. L. (1988). Excuses: Their effective role in the negotiation of reality. *Psychological Bulletin, 104*, 23-35.

———. (1990). Reality negotiation and excuse-making: President Reagan's 4 March 1987 Iran arms scandal speech and other literature. In M. J. Cody & M. L. McLaughlin (Eds.), *The psychology of tactical communication* (pp. 207-28). Clevedon, England: Multilingual Matters.

Snyder, C. R., Higgins, R. L., & Stucky, R. J. (1983). *Excuses: Masquerades in search of grace.* New York: John Wiley & Sons.

Stokes, R., & Hewitt, J. P. (1976). Aligning actions. *American Sociological Review, 41,* 838-49.

Street, R. L., Mulac, A., & Wiemann, J. M. (1988). Speech evaluation differences as a function of perspective (participant versus observer) and presentational medium. *Human Communication Research, 14,* 333-63.

Students step up protests on war. (1970, May 9). *New York Times,* 1.

Sullivan, A. (1989a, May 19). Exxon's holders assail chairman Rawl over firm's handling of Alaska oil spill. *Wall Street Journal,* p. A3.

———. (1989b, May 17). Protesters over Exxon handling of oil spill plan confrontation at annual meeting. *Wall Street Journal,* p. A8.

Sullivan, A., & Bennett, A. (1989, March 31). Critics fault chief executive of Exxon on handling recent Alaskan oil spill. *Wall Street Journal,* p. B1.

Suro, R. (1989, July 2). Tapes on Alaska's oil spill erased by Exxon technician. *New York Times,* p. 9.

Sykes, G. M., & Matza, D. (1957). Techniques of neutralization: A theory of delinquency. *American Sociological Review, 22,* 664-70.

Tedeschi, J. T., & Reiss, M. (1981). Verbal strategies in impression management. In C. Antaki (Ed.), *The psychology of ordinary explanations of social behavior* (pp. 271-326). London: Academic Press.

Ting-Toomey, S. (1994). *The challenge of facework.* Albany, NY: State University of New York Press.

Tracy, K. (1990). The many faces of facework. In H. Giles & W. P. Robinson (Eds.), *Handbook of language and social psychology* (pp. 209-26). Chichester: John Wiley.

U.S. House approves reforms: Members hope to clean up reputation. (1992, May 10). *Columbia Daily Tribune*, p. 14A.

Union Carbide. (1984, December 10). Text of statement by company on gas leak. *New York Times, 134*, p. A8.

Union Carbide executive charged with homicide. (1992, March 27). *Columbia Daily Tribune*, p. 3A.

Vangelisti, A. L., Daly, J. A., & Rudnick, J. R. (1991). Making people feel guilty in conversations: Techniques and correlates. *Human Communication Research, 18*, 3–39.

Vartabedian, R. A. (1985a). From Checkers to Watergate: Richard Nixon and the art of contemporary apologia. *Speaker and Gavel, 22*, 52–61.

———. (1985b). Nixon's Vietnam rhetoric: A case study of apologia as generic paradox. *Southern Speech Communication Journal, 50*, 366–81.

Vatz, R. E., & Windt, T. O. (1974). The defeats of Judges Haynsworth and Carswell: Rejection of Supreme Court nominees. *Quarterly Journal of Speech, 60*, 477–88.

Von Wright, G. H. (1971). *Explanation and understanding*. London: Routledge & Kegan Paul.

Ware, B. L., & Linkugel, W. A. (1973). They spoke in defense of themselves: On the generic criticism of apologia. *Quarterly Journal of Speech, 59*, 273–83.

Watzlawik, P., Beavin, J. H., & Jackson, D. D. (1967). *Pragmatics of human communication*. New York: Norton.

Webster blasts Post-Dispatch. (1992, August 13). *Columbia Daily Tribune*, p. 5A.

Weiner, B., Amirkhan, J., Folkes, F. S., & Verette, J. A. (1987). An attributional analysis of excuse-giving: Studies of a naive theory of emotion. *Journal of Personality and Social Psychology, 52*, 316–24.

Wells, K. (1989, May 17). Exxon captain's role in oil spill becomes clearer. *Wall Street Journal*, p. A8.

Wells, K., & McCoy, C. (1989, April 3). Out of control: How unpreparedness turned the Alaska spill into ecological debacle. *Wall Street Journal*, pp. A1, 4.

Westhead rejects blame. (1992, April 23). *Columbia Daily Tribune*, p. 2B.

William, D. E., & Treadaway, G. (1992). Exxon and the Valdez accident: A failure in crisis communication. *Communication Studies, 43*, 56–64.

Wilson, G. L. (1976). A strategy of explanation: Richard M. Nixon's August 8, 1974, resignation address. *Communication Quarterly, 24*, 14–20.

Witkin, R., Malcolm, A. H., & Suro, R. (1989, April 16). How the oil spilled and spread: Delay and confusion off Alaska. *New York Times*, pp. A1, 30.

Woody Allen denies molestation allegations. (1992, August 19). *Columbia Daily Tribune*, p. 8A.

Subject Index

Author Index

195